PLYMOUTH
PICTURES FROM THE PAST

Guy Fleming

DEVON BOOKS

First published in Great Britain in 1995 by Devon Books

British Library Cataloguing-in-Publication Data
A CIP Catalogue Record for this book is available
from the British Library

ISBN 0 86114 886 X

DEVON BOOKS
Official Publisher to Devon County Council

Halsgrove House
Lower Moor Way
Tiverton, Devon EX16 6SS

Telephone: 01884 243242
Facsimile: 01884 243325

Printed and bound in Great Britain by
The Devonshire Press Ltd., Torquay

~ CONTENTS ~

continues

~ FOREWORD ~
by
DAME JANET FOOKES DBE, MP
DEPUTY SPEAKER - HOUSE OF COMMONS

Like many other readers of the *Evening Herald* I was fascinated by the series of articles and pictures of bygone Plymouth and the inspiration of asking readers to identify them and give personal reminiscences. I am one of those who never knew pre-war Plymouth, but I can understand the affection and feelings of nostalgia that such pictures evoked. It sounds ridiculous but I am sure it is possible to feel an indirect nostalgia and this explains why the series so appealed to many younger readers.

Sadly, however, most people find it difficult to keep newspaper cuttings and I am delighted therefore that Guy Fleming has transformed the original concept into a book which will be easier to keep and to treasure. I have a high regard for Guy Fleming, both as a journalist who maintains the highest standards of his profession and as a man with an extensive knowledge of Plymouth. In his book, however, he has allowed individuals of all ages and types to speak of their own recollections and knowledge of the city in days gone by. The result is an intriguing mosaic of pictures and memories.

I shall certainly want to present a copy of the book to my mother. Although she did not know Plymouth in pre-war days she has always expressed the view very firmly that fascinating as places are, people are always more important. The charm of this book lies in bringing the two together.

Dame Janet Fookes DBE, MP
House of Commons, 1995

~ ACKNOWLEDGEMENTS ~

The author and publisher are grateful to all those, to numerous to name individually, who provided material for use in this book. Particular thanks are due to Keith Scrivener, Deputy Editor of the *Evening Herald* who suggested the original idea for the newspaper series 'Pictures from the Past'. Thanks also are due to Dame Janet Fookes for her kind interest and support. Finally, thanks to all those readers of the *Evening Herald* who, over the years, have shared their memories and made possible the publication of this book.

~ INTRODUCTION ~

It was one of those ideas that seemed to be good at the time, and proved to be. *Herald* Assistant Editor, Keith Scrivener, suggested trying a series of articles featuring pictures from the past, and asking readers to identify them. It might work, and it might not, he said. But, knowing Plymothian's penchant for nostalgia, he forecast that probably it would. As proved the case.

Over three years later, we are still receiving batches of memory-lane reminiscences from local people who, in some cases, have moved far away from their native city, but who love it and who want to keep in touch. Pictures of the city as they knew it has proved to be one of the most acceptable ways of maintaining their links. They knew, and yearned for, the throb of its daily heartbeat.

But this series has proved to be of interest not only to the 'oldies'. Surprisingly, perhaps, many younger readers have expressed appreciation of the pictures which give them a glimpse into a city which had a heart, real character and a certain amount of pathos. Certainly, the dwindling number of those who remember the pre-war Plymouth do so with an almost fierce love and loyalty which brooks no denial. They are deeply attached to it, and greatly mourn its passing. Nothing for them will ever replace the summer saunterings on the old pier, or moonlit strolls across the Hoe and to home after dancing the evening away in its confined but cosy ballroom. Horse-drawn trams from Hartley to the Theatre Royal and, of course, the much-loved old Devonport market also make up part of the fascinating mosaic of a city in which it was comfortable and easy to live.

The legendary whaft of roasted coffee from Goodbody's, in old George Street, has become almost the catalyst of deep nostalgia – that and the three-piece bands which used to play at several of the city's cafés, where you could still get a decent meal for 30p at 10pm.

It all came shuddering to a halt with dirgeful wail of sirens in 1941 and, as the old city was mercilessly destroyed, so its soul seemed to limp into oblivion. Its younger replacement, considered smart and invigorating at the time, has never eased away the memories of that more intimate city in which its people grew up, thankfully without many of today's ghastly social traumas, when they married, usually, 'for keeps' got a decent job and employed themselves with what may seem to us simple, easy abandon. Money often was tight, but community spirit was high and they kept their souls in good estate and were, by and large, a peace-keeping, lawful people, content to enjoy what to them was the ideal place to be. Then, as now, its people usually were glad to be back in Plymouth, after an absence.

It was of course, par excellence, a naval city and many memories reflect this. Devonport Dockyard at one time employed 20, 000 workmen to help look after the largest fleet in the world. Ships like the *Rodney, Hood, King*

George V, Resolution, not to mention the aircraft-carriers such as *Furious* and *Glorious*, were household names in and around Plymouth. So, too, were some of the world's great liners, like the *Isle de France*, the *Bremen* and the *Normandie*.

So, how do we explain this deeply-felt nostalgia? In fact, the intrigued 'outsider' shares it. Many have felt the magic pull which seemed to offer so much within such a short compass. Has it all gone forever?

Well, memories linger, but ultimately they die; which is why the responses from many hundreds of readers is an important piece of social history rather than a mere neighbourly verbal 'chit-chat'. Here is the stuff of which the people of Plymouth were made – the drama which surrounded their everyday lives, the conditions which generally they surmounted. They have unwrapped an amazing mosaic of the old city's former life, reminding us of a gentler, more at-ease age which had absolutely nothing to do with money or possessions: the days when an assistant would scrape a little finger across a butter mound to offer a customer a teaspoonful to taste before patting the required quantity.

A few went back a long way – even to the *feu de joie* spectaculars on Plymouth Hoe to commemorate Edward VII's birthdays. Many remember, with unconcealed glee, trips by train into the nearby countryside for six old pennies return; for seeing Gracie Fields at the Palace Theatre in the 'gods' at six old pennies a time – or, even earlier, watching Randolph Sutton in the pantomime at the Grand Old Theatre, its stage the biggest this side of Bristol.

Most children went, or were directed to, Sunday School where the annual outings were a treat to be anticipated all year. Often the destinations were places like Bere Alston or Cornwood – 'I think we imagined we were going halfway round the world,' one reader recalled.

Everybody's favourite stores, like John Yeo's, Spooners, Pophams and the more down-market Costers are constantly recalled Funny how seemingly slight incidents remain in the mind – the purchasing of button-up gaiters, either as a children or adults, is remembered by so many people.

Battershill's, the newsagents, Dilleigh's, The Three Towns Dairy, Underwoods and Vickery's are only a few of the smaller shops still fondly remembered by many who were their customers. All speak of alert and personalised service, a long-since lost trait in some.

So the roll-call went on and still does. There is a heart-cry for its continuance, yet logic dictates that one day, the barrel will run dry. Meanwhile, as the curtains on the past have been drawn back by so many readers, so a great deal of joy, and sometimes pain, has been released. Readers almost beg us not to stop, but encourage us to carry on, emphasising what a blessing it all is to them. So, for the forseeable future anyway, the cavalcade of memories must continue to roll. And why not?

Guy Fleming
Compton Gifford, 1995

~ MEMORIES OF OLD BEDFORD STREET ~

The photograph shows a rain-lashed Bedford Street in pre-war Plymouth. The Prudential Building, with its warm sandstone cladding, escaped destruction during the Blitz, but was taken down a few years after the war to allow Armada Way to be cut – much to the chagrin of many who wanted it retained.

The policeman on point duty would be coping with a great deal less traffic than nowadays; though, even then, the junction of Bedford Street and Old Town Street was said to be one of the busiest in the country.

Goodbody's cafe, on the left, was a popular venue for morning coffee and afternoon tea, with a three-piece band in attendance. A large bank and three big department stores were situated on the right of the picture: in this

Bedford Street, in the centre of pre-war Plymouth

first newspaper article readers were asked if they could remember their names. It turned out that many readers were familiar with pre-war Bedford Street. One even recognised the policeman on point duty as a relative, and several recalled working at Goodbody's cafe.

Mr Len Butt of St Dunstan's Terrace, St Jude's, recognised the policeman in our picture: it was his father-in-law, Charles Moss, then a well-known rugby player for Plymouth Albion and the City Police team. Mr Butt followed in his father-in-law's footsteps and controlled the traffic at Plympton before the bypass was built.

Mr Tony Dean of Wasdale Gardens, Estover, said that the policeman was directing traffic at the junction of Bedford and Westwell Streets and – in common with many other readers – he identified the two banks on the right as Lloyds and the National Provincial. The large department stores were John Yeo's, with the blind, and Dingles, just partly visible. Further east, but out of sight, were Pophams and Spooners.

Mrs E. Jordan of Kingsbridge was also one of many who wrote to say that the Westminster Bank is shown next to Goodbody's, on the opposite side of Bedford Street, and then came Dilleigh's, Stead & Simpson's and Liptons.

Shirley Wallis of Seaton, Cornwall, said that Bedford Street was Plymouth's most select shopping thoroughfare – 'and, in my memory, it was always bathed in sunlight. I remember being taken to Dingles. Children wore matching coats and hats, and I sometimes had gaiters as well, which required a button-hook to fasten.'

Mrs Wallis's grandmother, Mrs Lowe, was a well-known business-woman in the 1920s, who had a jewellery shop on the corner of Whimple Street and also owned the Gaiety Cinema in Union Street. 'On the corner of George Street, just opposite the Prudential, was a tobacconist called Salmon and Gluckstein. There my mother would buy her De Reske Minor cigarettes and change her library books at the back of the shop.'

Mrs Phyllis Andrews of Browning Road, Milehouse, worked as a cafe supervisor at Goodbody's, where she was employed for fifteen years. Romance struck for her there too: she married William Andrews, the violinist in the five-strong Stanton Wicks Orchestra, which played daily and was very popular.

'Goodbody's had several separate rooms, all beautifully decorated. The delicatessen and confectionery shops also were high-class and lots of people will remember the aroma of roasting coffee beans,' wrote Mrs Andrews.

Enid Ware of Rothesay Gardens, Crownhill, was a former waitress at Goodbody's where, she recalled, evening meals were served until 10 p.m. in the lower cafe. 'Upstairs, in the Oak Room lounge and Primrose rooms, we were busy from 10 a.m. to 6 p.m. The four-piece Stanton Wicks Band played for coffee, lunch and teas, up and downstairs on alternate days.'

Mrs Ware also recalled that the policeman who did point duty at Spooner's corner was nicknamed Punch because of his red, hooked nose.

'He was popular with everyone – such a nice, well-mannered man and so competent.'

Mrs Monica Voden of Crownhill Road was taken to Goodbody's with her two brothers for a special tea whenever her father sailed away on a commission in the Royal Marines. 'We would go to The Hoe to watch the ships sail and then back to Goodbody's for cream buns, chocolate eclairs or cream-filled sponge cakes. This didn't happen often as when Dad left it was usually for two-and-a-half years.' Mrs Voden later worked at the Prudential for a few months, in the income tax office, in the early days of the war.

Mrs Anne Randall of Farm Lane, Honicknowle, worked in the sewing room of Pophams store and left there to get married – a story in itself.

'I had my wedding reception at Goodbody's a week before war broke out in 1939. Arrangements had all been made and then I thought it would have to be cancelled because my fiancé was in the Regular Army. Anyway, he managed to get a twenty-four-hour leave and we were married at Holy Cross Church on August 20th. We spent the evening together and in the morning he had to return to the Citadel.'

Mr Robert Barwick of Southway Drive recalls that the Prudential was mainly face brickwork. 'I was an apprentice bricklayer at the time, and those I knew in the same trade always said it was the best face brick building in Plymouth. It was a tragedy when it was pulled down to make way for a new road.'

~ THE BLACK STOCKING BRIGADE ~

Scarlet blazers and hats, black knickers, flannel suits, buttoned gaiters made of leather or cloth, and the inevitable long stockings – that's what some readers remembered their parents buying for their school outfits from the outfitters Vickery's, shown in the picture of Bedford Street that appeared in the first newspaper article.

Elizabeth Deacon of Farm Close, Plympton, recalled that the bank seen on the right-hand side was originally the Devon and Cornwall Banking Company, which afterwards became Lloyds; the small turning beside it was Bank Street.

'I was a pupil at the Corporation Grammar School in North Road. We always had to buy our uniforms at W.J. Vickery, in Bedford Street. We wore scarlet blazers and hats with a gold badge, the Plymouth coat of arms. If we dared buy the uniform at any other shop there was trouble, because no other sold the exact shade of red.'

Mrs Vera Phillips of High Street, Stonehouse, was also taken to Vickery's for her black school stockings (double knees) and black knickers (double bottoms).

The former Devon and Cornwall Banking Company building in Bedford Street in 1908. This later became Lloyds and the head cashier was Mr John Foden, whose son, also John, became a Tavistock town councillor. The lane alongside the building was Bank Street. The picture gives a clear view of the advertisement for John Yeo's goods.

Alan Rowe of Great Mis Tor Close, Yelverton, was another one taken to Vickery's every year for his new, short-trousered flannel suit, ready for the Sunday School anniversary services in May. 'Later we went there for my school blazers and grey flannels.

'The old Dingles had long mahogany counters along each side of a fairly narrow gangway leading from the Bedford Street entrance into the interior. At frequent intervals there were bentwood chairs for the benefit of customers, laden with shopping and almost invariably obliged to stand while waiting for an assistant to appear. The bills were sent, with the cash payment, to a central cash desk via a pneumatic tube and, after a short interval, the container bringing the change and receipt would plop out into a box behind the counter. In Yeo's there was a different system of overhead wires which carried a round, wooden screw-up container, propelled by pulling a handle.'

Mrs Vera Deacon of Priory Road, Lower Compton, said that the Bedford Street shop owned by Underwoods was known as Trelawney House and the top floor was said to be haunted by the squire of that name.

'I worked for them for many years, and it was part of our initiation to be sent to the top of the building, which was very dimly lit. A water goods lift operated in the centre of the building, which we worked by pulling ropes to the various floors – the creaks and groans from this were certainly ghostly! We often opened the door to the lift well to come face to face with a rat making its way up the ropes.'

Mrs Dorothy Robinson's father, Mr F.T. Driver, was caretaker at the Prudential from 1924 onwards, living at the top of the much-admired building.

'The boiler for hot water was in the cellar, and so was the coal which he had to put into buckets and take by lift to the three floors. The Pru. was a lovely building. The staircase was a sort of spiral with a wooden banister rail. My brother and I used to slide down it; unfortunately, I overbalanced once and woke up in hospital with a fractured skull.'

Mrs Chambers from Eggbuckland spotted her bedroom windows in the picture of Bedford Street: they were on the attic at the very top of the John Yeo store.

'I was on the staff and, with six other girls and a housekeeper, lived above the store. During our off-duty time of an afternoon, and if the weather was good, we would go out on to the roof and, with envy, watch the lovely brides cutting their wedding cakes in the Goodbody's cafe which was opposite.'

'We entered through a door in Bank Street to get to our apartments, up a flight of stone steps, through several passages, up more stairs and so work our way across to Bedford Street. It felt very lonely in that big building alone.'

~ MUSIC AT GOODBODY'S ~

The picture of Goodbody's in Bedford Street brought memories flooding back to Mr Tony Haggitt of Leigham because his mother, Margaret, was the

Margaret Haggitt, for many years violinist in the Stanton Wicks Orchestra

13

violinist in the Stanton Wicks Orchestra there for many years. He added that she was a part of the Plymouth music scene for twenty years in the 1920s and 1930s.

'There must be many people who still remember her. A short lady with a fine head of frizzy hair, she always stood to play in front of the orchestra at Goodbody's. She loved her music and never took a holiday that I can remember. She was far too busy, for as well as playing at Goodbody's daily, she also provided the music at Genoni's Swiss Cafe, near Derry's Clock, every night.'

'Over the years she played also in the Palm Court at the Royal Hotel, in the Lockyer Hotel and with Albert Hosie's Orchestra in Spooners store. With a home to run and three strapping sons to bring up, my mother, who was a widow, carried an immense workload and was one of the jolliest people you could wish to meet. She died twenty-five years ago; I've always loved her music as much as she did.'

~ A ROYAL VISIT ~

The photograph shows Lady Astor visiting a new housing estate at St Budeaux in 1936. Readers were asked to identify the two men walking on either side of her, one of whom was a member of the royal family and the other the Lord Mayor of the day.

Mrs Mary Batter of Buller Park, Saltash, was the first reader to write in and she correctly named the figures as the Duke of Kent, who made several visits to Plymouth in the 1930s, and, on the right of the picture, Alderman Bert Medland.

Taken in 1936, this picture shows some well-known figures visiting St Budeaux.

14

The late Labour group leader Ron King pointed out that Mr Medland was elected as Plymouth's first Lord Mayor in 1935, having won a seat on the council in the Mount Edgcumbe ward in 1923. Bert Medland was Labour MP for Plymouth Drake for five years from 1945. He died in 1964, in his eighties and while still on the council. The resulting aldermanic vacancy was taken over by Mr King, who well remembers his predecessor.

'He was known as "Stormy" Medland, and worked well with Lord Astor in the reconstruction plans for the post-war city. He later became a strong advocate to retain the Guildhall, which many councillors wanted to demolish.'

~ BITTERSWEET MEMORIES ~

Two readers of the *Evening Herald* recalled the days when they used to queue up for any bits and pieces of left-over food which they could get for knock-down prices and which sometimes had to last their families for a week.

As a child, Mrs Doreen Roper of Erle Gardens, Plympton, used to be taken to a confectionery shop in Bank Street, just off Bedford Street, where her mother worked as a cleaner.

'She worked hard for just a few shillings when Dad was unemployed. I was the youngest of six children. I had to sit on a chair in the shop and not move until she had finished. It was agony looking at all the lovely sweets

This circular block was at the top of Old Town Street and noted for its optimistic neon sign: 'Guinness is Good for You.' It was demolished after the Second World War to make way for the much less pleasing Drake Circus precinct.

and chocolates. The owner, Mrs Parnel, never even gave me one; in fact, she hardly spoke except to tell my mother what she wanted her to do.

'After she had finished we went over to the market to Mr Soper's stall. There we went for four pennyworth of beef for pasties for all of us, some bones for soup and beef dripping; we loved that on a crust when we came home from school.'

Mr S.C. Quick of Claremont Street remembered the days, as a child, when he would ask for three pennyworth of scrap bacon from the much-loved Underwoods store, which he entered by the rear entrance in Cornwall Street.

'I went to the bacon counter where a short, stout man in white with a bald head, which used to shine, would tell me to stand at the end of the counter and wait. After he had served all the "gentry" he would wrap up all the bits and leftovers, and often I would go home with a nice parcel which would last us all week.'

~ A RIGHT CHARLIE ~

A horse that got loose but found its way home without any difficulty was recalled by Mr W. Hatherley of Quarry Park Road, Plymstock.

'During the 1920s and 1930s my father was a fish hawker and the proud owner of a horse and cart from which he plied his trade. One day, when he had finished his round, he stopped at Beers, the forage merchant in Russell Street, to buy some feed for his horse, Charlie. Mr Beer, the proprietor, and my father were good friends and often shared a few pints in the Starkey, Knight and Ford public house opposite. It was my father's custom before going to the pub to put the feed-bag on to Charlie, probably to pacify him.

'On this particular day the horse, tired of waiting, decided to make his own way home. It was second nature for him to proceed through Russell Street into Bedford Street and, even though driver-less, he was given V.I.P. access to St Andrew Street by the policeman on point duty. From there Charlie reached Castle Street with no trouble at all. Some time later my distraught father appeared at the top of the street, shouting, "Charlie! Where are you?".'

~ RECOLLECTIONS OF THE 'POPPET OF POPHAMS' ~

Gordon and Phyllis Foden of Whitchurch had good reason to remember the pre-war Plymouth store of Pophams, dubbed 'the Harrods of the West'. They met while serving as assistants in this much-loved shop which catered unashamedly for the 'county set' and the city's well-heeled people.

To be appointed as a salesgirl in Pophams in the 1930s was a mark of social distinction – the firm preferred girls who had been either to a convent

Autumn

POPHAMS
PLYMOUTH

Phyllis Foden posing on the moors for the autumn 1934 Pophams catalogue. The dog was borrowed from a nearby householder.

school or to Plymouth High, and the discipline was tough. Phyllis Foden started work in the glove department, at the beginning of a three-year apprenticeship.

'We weren't allowed to initiate conversations with the customers and, in a sense, were the lowest of the low. For all that, I very much wanted to be taken on at Pophams after leaving Notre Dame School, simply because of the prestige of the store, which catered largely for county people. My pay was 15 shillings a week, and we were the only firm to close on Saturday afternoons.'

Later Phyllis went into the jewellery department and sometimes she would catch snatches of the music being played by George East and his Trio in the large, lavish restaurant, 'and to have tea there was like going to the Savoy'.

Gordon's grandfather, Harcourt Foden, lived in Durnford Street, running his coal merchant's business off a wharf nearby, with an office in Bedford Street. His father, John, was the head cashier at the former Devon and Cornwall Banking Company, later Lloyds, in Bedford Street.

'He came to Plymouth from Exeter in 1909, the year after my grandfather died. His wife, Ethel, (my mother) was rather like old Queen Mary in bearing and demeanour, and she made a remarkable impact in Plympton. Apart from anything else, she raised thousands of pounds for the various hospitals, often by running immensely popular charity balls.'

Young Gordon, after leaving Plymouth College, packed his bags and went to London with £2 in his pocket, to try his luck. He had as his mentor the Tavistock MP, Brigadier General Wallace-Wright, VC. However, serious health problems in the big city forced him back to the balmier West Country climate, which is how he came to work at Pophams.

He began his career there selling silk to ladies, 'which I hated. I was a teenager and the store's owner, Alderman Sir Arthur Hollely, was a self-made man and a tyrant. Yet he was also a fair man: when he knocked you down he also picked you up again.'

Mr Foden stayed in the store, situated half-way along Bedford Street, for five years. It was both high class and expensive, with one of the finest furniture departments in the country.

'It was a wonderful institution, with three floors of high quality products. You never knew whom you might be serving: it might be the Countess of Mount Edgcumbe one moment and the Lord Mayor of Plymouth the next.'

Gordon Foden entered the lion's den of Sir Arthur's office and, in spite of the latter's brusque and dismissive manner, persuaded Pophams' owner to give him a chance to 'go on the road', selling the firm's merchandise.

'He growled his assent and one of the upshots was that I sold the first Aga cooker in the West Country. My job covered the whole of Devon and Cornwall, mainly selling to hotels.'

Mr and Mrs Foden took over the Whitchurch Inn some 24 years ago, and then the Virtuous Lady pub in Plymouth Road.

~ TAVISTOCK ROAD AND UNION STREET ~

All the buildings on the right in this photograph have gone – demolished not by bombs during the Second World War, but by demolition squads afterwards. The A386 sign on the lamp-post indicates that this is Tavistock Road and readers were asked if they could recall the shops on the other side.

Mrs Marian Matthews of Woodland Road, Plympton, identified the much-loved Harvest Home in the distance on the right, recalling that a dry-cleaners' stood on the corner. The name J. F. Hussell can be made out on the shop in the foreground and, jutting out beyond the shops, is part of the old City of Plymouth School of Art.

On the opposite side of the road was Yardley's music shop, 'where, in 1929, my mother bought me my first piano for £20,' recalled Mrs Matthews.

The photograph on the next page shows the crowds out in force on a pre-war summer's day. They were watching a car carnival wending its way down Union Street in the mid 1920s.

Albert Pengelly's the tobacconist's was on the corner of No. 1 Union Street and Bank of England Place, while further west was the old Oliver's boot and shoe shop.

Tavistock Road

A car carnival in Union Street

~ *DORA'S RINGSIDE VIEW OF LANDING* ~

Dora Wood was just into her teens when the First World War erupted in August 1914, and she vividly remembered the resulting turmoil and sense of shock this brought to her family and friends. When she talked to the *Evening Herald*, her memories of Plymouth before the 1914–18 war were still clear, as were those of the happy years she spent as a barmaid in the Repertory Theatre.

Young Dora started school at the tender age of three, in 1904, at the infants section of the old Public Secondary, then in Cobourg Street.

'My father had died and my mother had to go out to work, as a cook in the R.N. Hospital, Stonehouse. One of the first things I did there was to play in the sand-pit, although I did learn to read at a very early age.'

Dora was thirteen when the First World War began and the school moved to premises opposite the old slaughterhouse for its duration. The horror of that holocaust soon impinged on the minds of the pupils, sometimes in a bizarre manner.

'I remember children shouting in the street, "There are some wounded soldiers coming in at North Road Station." We all ran up York Street to watch them. They arrived in special hospital trains – scores of them. We saw some on stretchers, obviously badly wounded, others were walking, sometimes with difficulty. They were taken to what is now Devonport High School for Boys which was then the Military Hospital. Gradually we got used to it, and no longer rushed up to the station to watch them.'

In August, the month war broke out, 33 liners arrived in Plymouth Sound from Canada after one of the most extraordinary sea processions in history. They landed 25,000 volunteers in the Canadian Army in a manoeuvre which was a complete surprise to the Plymouth authorities, save for a handful at Admiralty House. The armada diverted here from Southampton after learning that German submarines were waiting for them near the Solent.

Dora had a ringside view of the thousands of troops who disembarked at the Millbay Skating Rink, later the site of the Ballard Institute.

'They climbed into the special trains waiting for them at the old Millbay Station, then the terminus for the GWR line from Paddington. They were a cheery, lively lot of men who waved to us, as we did to them. Little did any of us know that most of them were going to be killed at Vimy Ridge. It seemed such a waste of valuable young life.'

Meanwhile, the pupils at the public school in Tavistock Road were kept abreast of the war's progress, with teachers relating the latest episodes and describing the victories and defeats. Otherwise life continued much as normal for the young schoolgirl, one of whose pleasures was to romp around the reservoir parks at Sherwell and Hartley. Still, the war impinged on almost every aspect of her life. There was the great Zeppelin scare, when one of the sinister-looking floating monsters drifted slowly over Plymouth.

Later in the conflict rationing was introduced. 'We had to line up for our allowance of margarine, sugar, potatoes and many other vegetables.

A remarkable picture showing some of the Canadian soldiers who arrived in Plymouth in 1914. Mrs Wood watched them arrive from the site of the Ballard Institute, almost overlooking Millbay Docks.

We lived in James Street, off Tavistock Road, and I used to go up to Dilleigh's on Mutley Plain for our family rations. Rationing was similar to that which we all experienced in the Second World War, only it was more severe.'

Mount Batten was a hive of aerial activity and often Dora would watch the sea-planes sitting on its slopes, before they roared across the water and took off.

When at last the war finished in November 1918 Dora was going out with a handsome American sailor. Instead of joining the crowds celebrating the end of hostilities in the Guildhall Square, the two of them spent the evening at the former Andrew's Picture House, in Union Street, later revamped as the Gaumont.

'It was like bedlam even in there, though. No one really wanted to watch the film. Management kept inserting bits and pieces on the screen about what was going on outside. Union Street itself was packed with cheering, excited crowds, as the whole centre of town was. They were sticking notices in the windows of the *Evening Herald* offices, then in Russell Street, of the latest happenings. It was an intoxicating time, never to be forgotten, and it is still vivid in my mind all these years later.'

Mrs Wood was particularly interested in articles published in the *Herald* recently about the Repertory Theatre. She started work there as a barmaid in 1920 and knew the characters referred to, such as producer Edward Lockstone and stage carpenter Harry Hooper. But it was George King, the lessee, whom she particularly recalled, with great fondness and gratitude.

'He was a wonderful employer, and the staff all loved him. For instance, I went down to seven stone. Mr King said, "Dora, you are getting thinner than ever." He insisted I went to see his own doctor in Lockyer Street and then booked a fortnight's holiday for me in a lovely hotel at Yelverton. I came back to work a different person – that's the sort he was.

'Many famous people visited the Rep, including Sir Alan Cobham, who married one of the resident cast. Other visitors included – on their honeymoon – Lord and Lady Mountbatten.'

Mrs Wood's connection with the theatre went even deeper. Her father-in-law was the stage manager at the Palace Theatre for many years.

~ AUTOGRAPHS FROM DUNKIRK SURVIVORS ~

The first photograph shows Saltash Street in the late 1940s, taken from the north entrance near its junction with Pound Street. The lower picture was taken a few years before the Second World War and shows the east end of Union Street. When the pictures first appeared in the *Evening Herald* readers were asked if they could identify the mystery streets and name some of the shops.

All the buildings in this
picture of Saltash Street
have now gone.

Union Street in
the 1930s

Mr John Kitto, who ran a newsagency in the Money Centre precinct, was one of several readers who correctly identified the shops existing at that time in Saltash Street; his parents also ran a newsagency there, just where the street curved.

On the left, starting from the top, the shops were: a gift wholesalers; Edna Sherrell's; the Sugar Refinery public house; Staddon's bakery shop; Glanville's the butchers; Lovatt's the herbalists. On the right, starting from the bottom, were: a temporary food shop for Dingles; the Fifty Shilling Tailors; Dennings cooked meats shop; Coles coffee house; and Ray's the cycle shop.

Mr Kitto, ten at the time, can remember the Dunkirk survivors coming up the street in 1940, and he still has an autograph book with many of their names in it. His father bought him a new bicycle from Ray's for the princely sum of £2.99, and he used it to start a paper round.

'Mr Lovatt, our shop neighbour, also had a stall in the old market and I was paid a shilling to help push his barrow.'

Mr Kitto was a choir boy at the Central Hall, for which he was paid 7s. 6d. a quarter. Briggs' clothing club was next to the Hall, and then Trace's, a junk shop, followed by Fewing's, the hairdressers, where a haircut cost 1s. 6d.

Mrs Phyllis Partridge of Eastfield Avenue, Hooe, and a friend, started work in Saltash Street in 1945, when they left school. 'We both began on the same day, she at Arnold's seed shop and me at Willis's gown shop opposite. Next to it was the surgical appliance shop, Le Brasseur, and at the top of the street, on the corner, was a fruit and vegetable shop – Edna Sherrell's – where I worked for three years.'

Mr S. Robertson of Clarence Court remembered the Noah's Ark pub at the bottom of Saltash Street, with the top of Mill Lane also in view. He pointed out that Saltash Street connected Drake Circus to Cobourg Street and Mill Lane, which, in turn, led to the Sugar Refinery and Russell Street.

Mr George Baker of Peverell Park Road correctly estimated that the photographer must have been standing at the junction of Cobourg Street, Pound Street and Saltash Street, and that Gary's boot and shoe repair shop, on the left-hand side, would have been just out of view.

'The XL Dairy stood on the corner of Mill Street. I well remember that my mother would ask the assistant, "Is that butter fresh?" The assistant would scrape a little finger across the butter mound to offer her a teaspoonful to taste before patting up the required quantity.'

Mr Baker also remembered being bought a bicycle from Ray's cycle shop; it was a Bailey's roadster with Sturmey-Archer three-speed and Lucas dynamo – 'a combined birthday present and prize for passing the scholarship'.

Mr R. Baron of Sheridan Road, Manadon Vale, was one of several readers who worked for one or other of the shops shown in the pictures – only in his case it was two. He started at the Fifty Shilling Tailors, in Union Street, in 1933 when he left school and he also worked for Arnold's seed shop, in Saltash Street, for twenty years. He says that the tram coming towards the photographer in Union Street was a No. 2, bound for Peverell, and that it would shortly turn right into the Derry's Clock area.

Mr H. Finnimore of Swinburne Gardens, Manadon, in his eightieth year when he wrote, worked in a restaurant there when he was in his late teens. 'I used to go to Bugwoods ice factory in Palace Street for a block of ice to cool down.'

Mr Baker estimated that the photographer must have been standing outside Dunn's the hatters in Bank of England Place, near the junction of Frankfort Lane, Courtenay Street and Union Street.

'Williams' Cafe, behind the awning on the right, was reputed to serve delightful light teas. The H. Samuel's jewellers, beyond it, was the smaller of that company's two premises in Union Street. I remember standing, as a small child, enthralled by the Hornby railway lay-out in Halford's shop window in pre-Christmas days. Farther along, close to the overhead clock, was the entrance to Athenaeum Lane, where the BBC Plymouth broadcasts originated.'

~ CHARACTERS FROM THE OLD MARKET ~

This scene in the photograph on the following page showing the old pannier market was familiar to many people. The most evocative memories were supplied by Mr William Abrams – hardly surprising since he was its superintendent for many years.

He recalled the bustling and friendly atmosphere and held fond memories of many of the stallholders, among them Mr George Bradley and his wife, May. Other characters in the market included Mrs E. Walters, 'better known to us as "Twinnie Pullyblank".' Mr Abrams, of Hooe, attended the funeral of Mrs Walters' husband, Bill, a few years ago.

Among those trading in the market were Harry Heath with his general stall, while there were two fish stalls run by John Fletcher and Jack Finch. William Rowe, was a poulterer in the market.

Mr Abrams worked for the city council for forty-three years, of which ten were spent as superintendent of the market. His other duties included being keeper of the city pound and caretaker of the Corn Exchange.

Mrs K. Mills of Birchfield Avenue, Beacon Park, remembers seeing rabbits and chickens in cages down one side of the first aisle in the market, with a sweet shop and a stall selling Sunday School texts at the bottom.

'On Saturdays local farmers produced stalls. There were also others for shell fish, cockles and mussels which sold at 2d. a plate.'

~ *WESTWELL STREET REMEMBERED* ~

Westwell Street connected Princess Square to Bedford Street and also the narrow Basket Street, through which trams used to travel. Miss V. Churchill of Southwell Road, Crownhill, was particularly interested in this photograph on the page opposite.

'I can see, quite clearly, my late father's shop, Plymouth Fisheries, run by A.H. Churchill, until he was killed in the Blitz. Other shops in the picture include The Westwell Jewellers, Chocolate Box, Fosters and Hearders – both chemists – Roberts the florists, and Solomon Stephens the bakers.

'About midway up Westwell Street was the entrance to George Street Baptist Church, which was set back from the main road. One of my more pleasant memories was of The Three Towns Dairy where a lady called, I believe, Miss King, who had the most lovely auburn hair plaited into "earphones", used to dispense junket and cream. Pryor's Academy and Battershill's paper shop led on to the main GPO at the top of the street. At the far end was R. Humms & Co., motor sales.'

Part of Westwell Street with some of its shops

Other names in Westwell Street that sprang to Miss Churchill's mind were: Davis Keelers the opticians; C.W. Blundell & Co., wines and spirits; the Town Hall Vaults; Audrey Earle, fashions; Mr Strong the butcher; and the Embankment Motors. The Plymouth Repertory Theatre was just around the corner in Princess Square.

~ YOU DON'T FOOL WITH DOROTHY ~

By the time Queen Victoria died in 1901, Dorothy Whittley had been going to school for a year. In an interview with the *Evening Herald* she looked back on her long life with refreshing candour, not seeking to hide its 'pock marks', but relishing many of the events and people which made Plymouth such a happy place to live in at the turn of the century.

North Road School, Plymouth, in about 1904, by which time Dorothy Whittley at eight, had been a pupil in another, almost adjacent, school for four years. The pupils of the two schools saw a lot of each other, though officially on strictly segregated lines!

She hardly wilted – in fact, she didn't at all – after more than five hours of conversation spread over two visits. Her mind was razor-sharp still and her powers of recall daunting. A lady of definite views, she didn't bear fools gladly and indeed put them in their place with sometimes waspish innuendo. However, after ninety years on the Plymouth scene, she had more right than most to evaluate the significance of past events which, at the time, may have seemed earth-shaking, but which with hindsight appear to be of transient worth.

Bedford Street, one of Plymouth's most fashionable shopping thoroughfares, as it was in the days before the First World War when Dorothy Whittley and her family knew it so well.

One of her earliest memories was of the *feu de joie* spectaculars to commemorate Edward VII's birthdays. This involved hundreds of soldiers lining up to face the sea from Rame Head to Bovisand and, one after the other, firing into the air with their rifles. This drew expectant throngs every year and she could still remember the excitement, not to say the crack of thousands of rifles, at the 1903 *feu de joie*, when she was seven years old, by which time she was attending Caer Baden Private School in North Road.

Another treat for small girls soon after the turn of the century was to ride by horse-tram from Derry's Clock to Hartley. 'They were run by Baskerville's Transport. There were no recognised stopping-places; you had to indicate when you wanted to get off and, likewise, anyone could hail the horse-tram, in the manner of waving down a taxi. The trams were drawn by two horses and they were lovely great brutes. Such trams also ran around The Hoe front and we would sit upstairs, in the open, back to back.'

Trips into the nearby countryside were also popular ninety years ago, such as Plymouth to Yelverton for 6d. return. 'It was an evening run and the trains would be packed, often by people who had been working all day. They would have a good walk around the moors and then catch the last train to Plymouth, at 9.30 p.m., though there were earlier ones too. Others would go on to Princetown – a really lovely run over the moors. We used to call this the 'Woolworth train' because it cost only 6d. Another trip was to Plympton, calling at Marsh Mills Station, 3d. each way.'

Dorothy Whittley was born in Lisson Grove, Mutley, and has lived there all her life. Her father founded Rotary in Plymouth and became a noted philanthropist. She left school at seventeen and – so she says – 'just mucked around until the First World War turned up'.

The outbreak of war was a call to arms for the 18-year-old Dorothy. She joined the Devon 86 Red Cross and was appointed secretary at a hospital for army officers in the converted Hyde Park School.

One of the annual *feu de joie* spectaculars commemorating Edward VII's birthday; this photograph was supplied by Mrs G. Hooper of Highclere Gardens, Roborough.

'They went there direct from the Red Cross ships, dressed in their uniforms which sometimes were caked with filth. On occasion, their trousers, when taken off, would stand bolt upright, they had that much mud on them – it was frightful. I had to be there whenever the convoys came into Millbay Docks, sometimes twice a day. There were hundreds at a time and I used to think "poor devils". As the battles at the Front grew fiercer and more frequent so we would get more of them and it was a heart-rending experience.

'The First World War was harder to go through than the Second, simply because no one knew how, or when, it was going to end until the final few weeks in 1918. I never thought our men would fight as they did. They put up a wonderful show, you know, and there was never a scrap of trouble from them in the hospital; they were gentlemen in the true sense of that word.'

Miss Whittley's great love through life has been BUPA. She joined in 1923, thinking at the time it was 'one of those silly little associations that were about'. She was to become its secretary for half of Devon and all of Cornwall for twenty-seven years, and it became her full-time occupation. 'I was so absorbed in my work that I didn't have time for much in the way of pleasure-seeking or holidays, and I was still active in it until the age of seventy-eight.'

Miss Whittley was one of the driving forces behind the present Nuffield Hospital at Derriford; perhaps the principal one. 'I was told a nursing home in Plymouth would never pay, and that used to make me angry. The people in London didn't have much idea of how things worked down here, so I told them: "Look, I have got all these people to join and they have nowhere to go." Eventually the headquarters people were driven into building the Nuffield. I had told them that if they didn't do something, and quickly, they could have my resignation there and then. Well, as everyone knows, it opened in 1972, and I'm jolly glad.'

That was Dorothy Whittley – to the point and decisive.

~ MEETING AT SPOONER'S CORNER ~

These two photographs of well-known locations in Plymouth were easily recognised by many readers of the *Herald*, who wrote in with their memories of the streets in times past.

Mr S. Robertson worked at the *Evening Herald* offices before the war, so he knew the area shown in the top photograph particularly well. He pointed out that the road on the right joined George Street and Bedford Street. A policeman was standing at the junction, and Mr Robertson noted that Russell Street is on his left: 'The corner shop on the left was Oliver's boot and shoe shop.'

The junction of Frankfort Street and Cornwall Street, taken from a spot near the *Evening Herald* offices; the policeman on point duty had a busy time, as did the pedestrians trying to jostle their way past the shops.

St Andrew's Corner, more commonly known as Spooner's Corner, crowded and congested even on 'slack' days; this photograph was taken in 1937.

In the lower photograph he correctly identified the junction of Bedford Street, Old Town Street and Whimple Street. The old Western National office was on the corner of Whimple Street and he recognised the spot from which the picture was taken as Bateman's the opticians. He ought to know – he painted the scene many times on canvas!

Mrs Pat Kingdon of Taylor Close, Burraton, pointed out that the trams and buses seen in the second picture were coming from and going to Basket Street. Balkwill's the chemists can be seen facing the photographer. Mrs Kingdon added that she thought Plymouth had a lot more character in those days.

Most readers – Mrs P. McHaffie among them – remembered that Vickery's the outfitters is shown in the first picture; the shop was later to be taken over by Dingles. Mrs McHaffie, of Old Laira Road, had particular reason to remember Spooners because she worked in its fashion department.

'I loved every minute of it. That's when a fashion floor looked beautiful – not like present-day stores with everything pushed together on the rails. I still have fashion photos of models on The Hoe in 1920 – all Plymouth girls, as I was too. We would do fashion parades in the store's theatre and sometimes at the Guildhall.'

Mrs Edith Knapman of Craven Avenue, St Judes, remembers her mother buying her first school uniform for what was then Devonport Secondary School (now the High) in 1926. 'With school blouses at 4s. 11d. each (about 25p), and wages about £2 a week, two would be a luxury, and a rip in one of them would be a catastrophe.'

Mrs Kathleen Mills of Birchfield Avenue, Beacon Park, in her reminiscences of pre-war Plymouth, said that in those days 'we were safe in the parks and streets from muggers, even if there was poverty and low wages'.

~ THE THEATRE ROYAL AND HA'PENNY GATE ~

Not many readers were old enough to be able to recall these two pictures, as many correspondents pointed out. Even so, a lot of people correctly spotted the old Theatre Royal, taken in the early years of this century. The photograph triggered many fond memories of theatre-going before the war. The theatre was eventually demolished in 1937.

The other photograph shows Stonehouse Bridge – or Ha'penny Gate, as it was always known. The photograph was taken in the 1920s.

Many people had good memories to share about one or other of the two sites. The fullest description came from former *Evening Herald* copytaker Tom Winzor of Herschel Gardens, King's Tamerton, who wrote that the series of pictures brought back memories, 'good and bad'.

He had memories of a particular horse and cart on Stonehouse Bridge, probably a Great Western Railway or Pickford delivery van. 'In the 1920s and 30s horses and carts used the bridge in abundance and no one had a better selection than the hundreds held by the Co-operative greengrocery

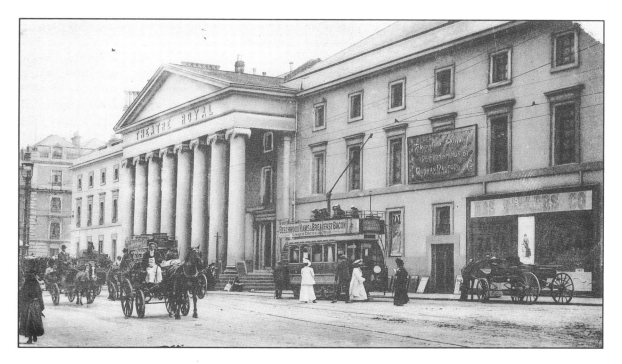

and bakery shops. Their wagons were specially made not only to carry goods on the side trays, but also inside to save returning to the depot for refills.

'The bridge had water flowing underneath and it was possible to boat up to Millbridge. During the two world wars this was a busy waterway and many a hospital boat would run beneath the bridge, full of casualties bound for the Royal Naval Hospital or the British Military Hospital – Devonport High School today. At one time the creek ran from Stonehouse up to Pennycomequick, to the point where the GPO's sorting office now stands.'

Mr S. Robertson pointed out that the use of Stonehouse Creek was curtailed in late 1941 when a dam was built under the bridge to create a large static water tank for fire fighting. 'Prior to 1939 the creek did fall a little short of Millbridge and, at that time, you would not attempt to row very far past this because of the mudbanks.'

Mr Winzor also recalled that the tram routes running across the bridge were, among others, the Nos 1 and 2 circular routes traversing Mutley Plain, Peverell, Milehouse, Stoke, Devonport and Union Street.

He also remembered the Royal Hotel, next to the Theatre Royal, for he and his elder brother used to play snooker or billiards there. NAAFI nissen huts were later put on this site.

R.J. Ward of Downfield Drive, Plympton, saw his first pantomime, *Babes in the Wood*, at the Theatre Royal around 1922. He recalled a series of pillars and gates near the theatre at the entrance to The Crescent, in

Millbay Road. He remembered catching the No. 16, bound for Lower Compton, from the bus stop outside the theatre.

Mr Ward certainly remembered escapades on Stonehouse Bridge. 'As a young boy, I managed to hop on the back of a cart many a time, hide under the sacks or whatever in the back, and get across without paying!'

Elizabeth Deacon pointed out that the Royal was designed by John Foulston the architect, who came from London early in the last century and who, she says, completely changed the face of Plymouth. 'The theatre seated 1,192 people. It had its own scene-painting room and machinery for quick changing, and the entertainment was very varied, from musical comedy to opera and traditional Christmas pantomime.'

She also recalled there being three toll gates in Plymouth at one time, the other two being at Millbridge and the Embankment. 'At Stonehouse the toll for a cart with one horse was 2d., rising proportionately. Foot passengers were charged one halfpenny, hence the name Ha'penny Gate. Young boys used to run through on the blind side of the trams or carts to avoid paying the toll.'

Mr F. Young of Durris Close, Thornbury, remembered there being a number of toll gates in the city, including three on the Embankment. He said that one was situated at the town end beside the Corporation Grammar School playing field, another was at the Lanhydrock Road junction and the third at the Laira end.

'There was also one on the Iron Bridge, over the River Laira, and we youngsters went across the railway bridge to save a ha'penny. The toll gates were freed on 1 April 1924, when Solomon Stephens was the mayor; we all had a day's holiday from school.'

Stonehouse Bridge, otherwise known as Ha'penny Gate

Stan Robertson said that his aunt lived in the top floor of the building seen standing behind the granite tollhouse on the bridge, and a dentist occupied the ground floor. The building at the far end of the bridge on the left was, he said, a public house; the landlord was Putty Philpott, allegedly the fattest man in the Navy at one time.

◘   ◘   ◘

~ SEA AND BOATS WERE SAM'S LIFE ~

When Sam Webber's grandfather was born near Stonehouse Creek the Royal William Victualling Yard was a gleaming new marvel. Sam's father first saw the light of day in the same spot and so did he, just before the turn of the century. When he gave this interview to the *Evening Herald* a few years ago he was ninety-two.

Sam was one of the best-known and loved boatmen in the city, retiring from the business only when he was eighty-six – and then under protest. He grew up with the sight and smell of the sea and boats and never really wanted anything else. So attached were Sam and his family to the Creek that, some years ago, he couldn't have found his way to Mount Gould or Ford, and of Plymouth's social world he knew nothing and cared less. Even his regular sorties into The Barbican were only to buy bait.

Sam was born in his parents' home on the south side of the Creek's foreshore, just yards from where he lived in retirement, in the aptly named Anchorage, along Richmond Walk. When he was six, he was sent to a private school at Mutton Cove, not far away, and then on to Stuart Road school.

He did many different jobs in the years that followed, all of them connected with the sea and boats; he spent fourteen years as a professional fisherman, for instance. He earned his all-important boatman's licence at the exceptionally early age of sixteen and, at one time, had twenty boats which he leased out to those who wanted a row up and beyond the river. He was following in his father's and grandfather's wake – it seemed the most reasonable and natural thing to do. 'I never wanted to do anything else,' he said.

When he was a lad there were only twenty houses in Richmond Walk and the traffic was a few horses and carts clip-clopping their way up and down. 'It was as if we were all related. There was never a shade of animosity between any of us and we all helped each other. For instance, someone would gather firewood from the slipway, chop it up and distribute it around.

'If a woman was going to have a baby, each one of the mothers would be there to do their turn and help in whatever way they could. When a woman lost her husband she was compelled to go out to work because what was then known as her "parish pay" was only 2s. 6d. a week. We experienced real poverty in those days.'

Sam, a man given to many salty oaths, was all the time building up his business, leasing his boats, which were between 12 ft and 18 ft long, for 6d. an hour.

'People took pleasure in just having a row around. Of course the water flowed under Stonehouse Bridge up to the Royal Naval Hospital. Actually, it went even further – right up to Pennycomequick, by the GPO sorting office, though you couldn't row that far. Some people would go as far as Calstock. It took them five hours. They would go ashore for a cup of tea and then come back on the high water. This was particularly popular on a Bank Holiday. Often two fellows would go with a couple of girls for the day and it would only cost them 10s. Others would row to Millbrook Lake or over to Mount Edgcumbe.'

Fishing was the basic industry in those parts and Sam remembered wives going around to sell the fish their husbands had caught the previous night, at 3d. apiece. 'I gave away more fish than I have eaten. Sometimes I would come home with a catch of 300 mackerel from Newton Ferrers and give it all away.'

Of course Stonehouse Creek was a busy place 85 years ago, before so much of it was reclaimed the other side of the bridge. Barges, steamships and coal boats were frequent visitors, discharging their cargoes to the appropriate firms which then flourished in the district. Timber ships from Russia also called regularly. Brick firms operated locally and a joinery company employed eighty joiners.

Sam's one leisure pursuit was to trek up to the Devonport Library, then in Cumberland Street, where he read what he called his pet paper, *The Truth*, which exposed what its staff saw as rampant injustices.

He even found time to marry – though the courtship lasted ten years! 'Yes, I saved up so that my sweetheart, May Warren, would not go short if anything happened to me. We did plan ahead in those days.' The couple eventually married in 1930. Mrs Webber's father was a boat-maker and she was adept at helping her husband run the business. She died in 1980.

There was an armaments factory on nearby Ocean Quay years ago and the South-Western Railway Company ran trains through to London. Three tenders would often land passengers from transatlantic liners and during the First World War troops landed there. Wounded soldiers were taken upstream to the Royal Naval Hospital and this became such a common, if sorry, sight that local people hardly noticed it after a time.

All through those early years, however, Sam and May were conscious of the raging poverty that was Stonehouse, just over the bridge. 'The courtyards in High Street were indescribable. Two people would live in one room in their surrounding hovels, and there had to be regular days for doing washing, split up into clearly defined hours for each householder. Too bad if it rained! There were no handrails on some of the landings and one chap I knew used to haul himself up by a rope.'

So Sam was one of the old brigade who did not believe that the days of eighty years or so ago were invariably the best.

~ *GEORGE STREET AND ROYAL PARADE* ~

Readers were asked if could identify the two streets shown in the photographs on this and the following page, and name some of the shops. This proved to be an easy task for many people.

Mrs Elizabeth Deacon correctly identified the thoroughfare leading from Derry's Clock as George Street, with the Prudential building at the very top corner. She pointed out that Barber's, which can be seen in the picture, was a high-class gents' outfitters; after it was bombed it moved to The Crescent.

'Goodbody's had a small cafe at the bottom of George Street in addition to their larger one in Bedford Street. There was also Moon's the piano shop, Smarts furnishers, and Lympany the umbrella shop – the concert pianist Moura Lympany was a member of this family.'

Ray Davies, in company with Mrs Deacon and other readers, had no difficulty in identifying the new Royal Parade in the other picture and the store jutting out on the right as being the Co-operative Society's furnishing emporium in Courtenay Street. He said that this was opened for business on Wednesday, 16 November 1932.

'Right in the centre of the picture are two shops, in splendid isolation. They were 190 and 191 Union Street and were, respectively, Levy & Slogget and the Halford cycle company. In the background, slightly to the left of

The well-known landmark of Derry's Clock

This photograph of Royal Parade in its infancy was taken as recently as 1948.

the shops, is the Continental Hotel and on the skyline, to the right, are the Valletort Mills of Hosken, Trevithick, Polkinhorne & Co. Ltd, in Millbay Road.'

Spooners department store decorated for the Coronation of King George VI in 1937

Mr Davies enthused about the variety and quality of the shops in George Street, including the department store of Costers at its east end, together with restaurants, wine stores, hatters, umbrella makers, picture framers, boot and shoe shops, confectioners, tailors, hairdressers, watchmakers, furriers, a church (George Street Baptist) and a pub. 'It was a veritable shoppers' paradise.' He also mentioned that Derry's Clock, erected in 1862–63, cost just £720.

Mr D. Neoke of Ruskin Crescent recalled that the old Theatre Royal and St Catherine's Church were near Derry's Clock, leading up to Lockyer Street and The Hoe.

Referring to the photograph of Spooners department store in Old Town Street, Mr Neoke said that as you came into nearby Basket Street you could catch a D bus to Mount Gould. 'The tram driver would get out of the front of the tram and change points in order to go through Westwell Street.'

~ TIMES PAST IN DEVONPORT ~

Many readers remembered the Royal Sailors' Rest and some had vivid personal memories of that huge block which dominated the corner of Fore Street and Catherine Street. The other mystery photograph was easily identified as Fore Street, though only one reader mentioned the brand-new Forum cinema on the far right of the picture.

Mr S. Robertson had good reason to remember also the post office in Fore Street because his grandfather was the landlord of the Army and Navy pub a few doors down, and those were the days when sailors wore straw hats. His list of local shops included Marks & Spencer, whose building still

The Royal Sailors' Rest, or 'Aggie Weston's', was a prominent building in Devonport before the war.

stands inside the Dockyard, Tozers, Boots, Woolworths and, out of view, the Electric cinema, with the newly opened Forum cinema clearly in sight.

Mr S.M. Searle of Mudge Way, Plympton, pointed out that the wine merchants Saccone & Speed were on an opposite corner and that, on the right of the picture, is Barclay's Bank, where the Rev. Peter Bolt, who retired from the Methodist ministry, worked as a teenager.

Mrs Elizabeth also had good reason to remember the post office – she was a telephonist there from 1938 to 1942. She recalled that the classical building was modelled on the Temple of Tivoli. 'The site was originally that of a butcher's shop and the main doorway was reputed to have had the head of a bullock carved into it.'

She said that the post office opened in 1849 and the extension into Chapel Street was built in 1914. On the night of 20 April 1941, the building was split from top to bottom by a high-explosive bomb and the following night was gutted by fire.

Mrs Kathleen Mills remembered that the post office was opposite the gas company's office. She named several of the nearby stores and shops, including the Co-op drapers, Underwoods groceries, Hockings the piano and music shop, Singers, David Greigs and J. Tozers.

Many readers recognised the Royal Sailors' Rest, or 'Aggie Weston's', whose solid plinth stood outside the Fore Street entrance to the Dockyard until it was bombed. This was opened by the indomitable lady after whom it was nicknamed, in 1889, offering 900 cabins to sailors ashore.

Mrs Mills said that she benefited from its social work. 'The wives meeting was held on Monday afternoons, run for many years by Dame Sophia Wintz, for some time Miss Weston's close companion. Miss Carder was in charge of the library, a thrift club, social evenings and Christmas parties. Adults and children all got a present wrapped in newspaper. On Good Friday evening we went to see the Magic Lantern slides – a real treat indeed.

Fore Street, probably the busiest thoroughfare in pre-war Devonport; the photograph was taken in 1939.

'When Dame Sophia died we went to her funeral which was a full naval affair, with band and gun-carriage. We walked to Weston Mill cemetery and back; I was about ten years old at the time.'

Russell Wootten worked at David Sale's, opposite Aggie Weston's. He remembered that in those days they had a resident plumber and apprentice to attend to the boiler to heat the building. 'I was fire-watching on the premises, in the attic, on the night much of Fore Street was destroyed in the Blitz. Both Sale's and Aggie Weston's were bombed.'

Mr Wootten, of Frensham Avenue, Glenholt, presented to the city museum a teaspoon with the letters 'RSR' (Royal Sailors' Rest) embossed on the handle, as well as a 1936 catalogue from Halford's cycle shop then in Union Street.

~ WELL-KNOWN SHOPS OF THE PAST ~

A number of Plymouth's present residents worked in one or other of the shops shown in these photographs, now all demolished. The old General Post Office in Westwell Street was a well-remembered feature, as was the Guildhall with its prominent tower.

Mrs K. Hutchings of Seymour Road, Plympton, had good reason to remember Perkin's shop in Westwell Street since she used to work there. 'I well remember seeing the King and Queen from the first-floor window on their visit to Plymouth on the day of the big Blitz in March 1941.'

Old Town Street, looking towards Drake Circus, which disappeared only some years after the last war; this picture was taken some time between the two world wars.

Westwell Street, looking in the direction of The Hoe, with the GPO on the right and the Guildhall tower prominent in the distance

She also remembers Churchill's the fishmongers, the confectionery owned by Alderman Solomon Stephens, one of the city's chief Liberal figures and a Lord Mayor. 'My father often took me for junket and cream at the neighbouring Three Towns Dairy.'

Another reader claimed that either the Midland or Lloyds Bank occupied part of the YMCA building, and that on the other side of the GPO were Battershill's the newsagents, The Three Towns Dairy, Churchill's the fishmongers and then came Westwell Gardens. On the other side of that,

One of the best-known views of Plymouth before the Blitz – St Andrew's Cross; the cross on top of the monument now stands in the north aisle of St Andrew's Church.

and fronting Princess Square, was the Repertory Theatre. This anonymous reader said that he worked at the GPO from 1922 to 1929 and married one of the clerks.

On the floor of the old GPO building was a large mosaic depicting Sir Francis Drake and the points of the compass. The trees visible further down the street, near the Guildhall, are still there, but now of course outside the Civic Centre.

Mr S. Robertson was another reader who recalled these pre-war street scenes. He pointed out that Old Town Street boasted many well-known shops, such as Woolworth's, Le Brasseur, Notcutt the photographers, Stones and a Mumford's showroom.

The road leading off to the right from Old Town Street was Treville Street, where the Labour Exchange near Charles Church could be found. At its north end was the junction of Ebrington Street, Tavistock Road, Saltash and Cornwall Streets. Mr Robertson believed that the last tram to run in Plymouth left here for Mutley Plain.

~ QUEUING FOR HOURS TO SEE GRACIE FIELDS ~

Dozens of *Herald* readers were able to identify the buildings surrounding Derry's Clock in the photograph below. The late Geoff Reburn of Eton Place recalled that they included St Catherine's Church, Truran's tobacconist and confectionery shop and the Lockyer Hotel. The pillared building opposite was of course the Royal Hotel. Mr Reburn also mentioned that behind the clock were the beginnings of Union Street, looking out on Bank of England Place.

Taken in the 1920s, this photograph shows some of the substantial buildings in the vicinity of Derry's Clock at that time.

Union Street, with some of its many shops, before it was reduced to rubble in 1941; in the distance can be seen the former Gaumont cinema.

Union Street, seen in the above photograph, boasted about twenty pubs, five cinemas and two theatres in the years between the two world wars, Mrs Edna Williams recalled.

'I remember seeing Gracie Fields at the Palace after queuing several hours for the "gods", where we sat in great discomfort on wooden benches, for the price of 6d. We saw Randolph Sutton in the pantomime at the Grand Theatre and his song 'On Mother Kelly's Doorstep' was a great favourite.'

Mrs Williams, in her eighty-seventh year when she wrote in to the *Herald*, said that the largest of the many pubs in Union Street was the 'Long Room', where the barmaids all wore long black dresses. 'It was a common sight to see and hear the large dray horses carrying their barrels of beer to the numerous pubs. Those beautiful horses, all perfectly groomed, were housed in large stalls under the railway bridge which used to span Union Street.'

G.M. Williams from Kingsbridge worked at Currys, whose premises were in Athenaeum Lane, off Union Street, for eight years in the 1920s. 'The hours were from 9 a.m. to 8 p.m., with one hour allowed for lunch and 45 minutes for tea, and the wages just 7s. a week. Wireless was quite new then and you could rent or buy one for 2s. a week.'

Paul Stebbing of St John's Drive, Hooe, wrote to say that his grandfather opened a boot shop, and its accompanying warehouse, at No. 58 Union Street in 1870. 'The warehouse was used for making the upper parts of boots, machined by girls. The shop supplied pieces of leather for the men, who, in those days, mended families' boots and shoes themselves.

A thriving trade was also done in clogs, waxed leather uppers, beach soles and clog irons, worn by tram drivers who used to stop outside the shop and nip in for a pair. Girls from the Starkey & Knight breweries, at The Octagon, would clatter through Union Street in their clogs.'

Mr C.F. Pick of Cheltenham Place began his working life in Union Street in 1936, at the age of fourteen. It was at a specialist tool outlet with the G.W.R. stables sited conveniently at the rear; at that time all deliveries were made by horse and cart. Mr Pick remembers such nearby businesses as Johnson Lethbridge, the Wellington public house, the Empire cinema, A R Wallpapers, the Farley Hotel and, further up the road, Levy & Slogget, Halfords, Burtons, Posada, Jerome & Singers, among many others.

Referring to the Derry's Clock picture, Mrs Elizabeth Deacon recalled that St Catherine's Church was something of an austere building. It had a gallery with a large painting over the altar by Benjamin Haydon, a Plymouth artist who produced some of his most famous pictures in a debtors' prison. 'When St Andrew's Church was destroyed in the last war the congregation moved to St Catherine's and so did the famous city organist, Dr Harry Moreton.'

Mrs Deacon said that the Royal Hotel was the leading one in the West of England. 'Much of its clientele came from the great liners which anchored in the Sound; at one time it had a fleet of courtesy coaches drawn by horses. The hotel's Regency-style ballroom was 76 ft long and the Palm Court, decorated in white and gold, was famous for its afternoon tea and its orchestra.'

Mr S. Robertson started his working life as a waiter at the Royal, in the grill room. Eventually he left because he didn't like finishing work after midnight. He then took up employment at the Army and Navy Stores in Union Street, opposite Dankworths the dentists, the Admiral's Locker pub and the Empire cinema which, he said, was the smallest that side of Devonport. 'You entered under the screen. It was a single-aisle cinema with about eight seats on each side.'

He also remembered that situated on the corners of The Octagon were the Antelope Inn, Jay's the furniture store, the London furniture store and Pengelly's tobacco shop.

M.A. Shreeve of Southdown Road, Beacon Park, was a boy chorister at St Catherine's from about 1921-23. The adjacent wall, he said, enclosed the playground for the church's day school, which he attended. 'There was one teacher for the whole group of boys, ranging from standard one to seven. Although sharing the same playground, the boys and girls were not allowed to converse with each other.'

Mr Shreeve also has reason to remember the Royal Hotel because he and other choirboys helped to move some of its furniture when a fire broke out one Sunday morning around 1922.

~ MEMORIES OF PLYMPTON ~

Readers were asked if they could remember any of the shops in Ridgeway, one of Plympton's main streets. A large number of Plymptonians responded with long lists of the shops they remembered. Some of these lists contradicted each other, but among the premises clearly remembered were (on the left looking up): the Blue Bird Cafe, International Stores, the Midland Bank, Griffin's bun shop, Rattenbury the ironmongers, Dewhursts the butchers, Plymouth Dairies, the Bar-Lock typewriter repair shop, Deebles the electricians, Brock's the hairdressers, Wilcox sweet shop, Mrs McArthur the florists, Reggie Trickett the newsagents, Revells the butchers, Stevens antiques shop, Worth's fish and chip shop, Jane Lewis the hat shop, Burton's fruit shop, Kirkness the chemist, Mrs Gent's sweet shop, Underwoods the grocers, and Nickells the tobacconist.

On the other side, among many other premises, were: Hugh Phillips the chemist, Rhodes the grocer, Westrew's wool shop, Hefford's boot and shoe shop, Studley the ironmongers, Parnell the furnishers, Matthews the barbers, Mrs Slee's pet shop, Jackson's the butcher, Mrs Barnard's and Mrs Hodge's gift shops, the Peter Pan sweet shop, Scoble & Wills the grocers, and Burt's radio shop.

Mr George Baker remembered some of the shop owners, such as Mr Joyce, manager of the International Stores, who was a 'tall and very smart gentleman. Indeed, all staff were well turned out, in white starched coats and aprons.'

Norman Willis now of Chelmsford, Essex, confirmed that at one time Ridgeway was known as Fore Street, though other readers disagreed with this. He said that he had a photograph dated 1894, in the Francis Frith series, captioned 'Fore Street, Plympton St Mary'.

Ridgeway, Plympton, around 1914

The upper end of
Ridgeway, Plympton,
soon after the turn
of the century

He added: 'I was born in a house three doors down from the Wesleyan Chapel in 1914, when the title "Fore Street" was in general use. It occurs in some family legal correspondence dated 1936.' He said that part of Ridgeway was in the parish of St Maurice and his house was on the boundary.

Mr Willis supplied a list of traders from an earlier date than those given above. These included: Alfred Deeble the tailor (father of Charles the electrician), Mr and Mrs Heathman of Newnham Dairies, W. Andrews, greengrocer, George Ware, butcher, Ralph White, blacksmith, and Harry Stephens, baker. He also mentioned that there was a ropewalk behind the tall property on the right.

~ THE VILLAGE WITHIN A CITY ~

Many people remembered Compton Gifford with affection and with nostalgia for the pace and ethos of this close-knit community.

Tom Brock of Carbeile Road, Torpoint, attended the village school in Lower Compton from 1927 onwards, when the headmistress was a Miss Cox, who lived opposite the premises next to the Compton Inn.

He identified the photograph as taken from the foot of the steps leading up to Fortescue Avenue and Hartley. 'The shop in the top right of the picture was owned by the Baker family. My family lived in Priory Lawn Terrace, near the dairy. I have many memories of the village and its surroundings before the Efford estates were built and Blandford Road came into existence.'

Compton Gifford,
often described as 'the
village within a city'.

R. Wyatt of Channel Park Avenue, Efford, recalled that local builder Mr Hosking lived in the house next to the lamp-post and that farther down, on the right, was a small shop owned by Mr and Mrs Evans.

'A cobblers' shop was next door to the Compton Inn, and the post office, further down the road, was run by a Mr and Mrs Chapman. Mr Sam Daw's dairy was around the corner and so was Mr Tom Daw's dairy. I was born at 2 Blandford Road. My mum and dad, and gran and grandad, lived there all their lives.'

Another person who grew up in the village was Nigel Norris, called David by everyone when he was a lad. 'I can recall Harry and Violet Leatwood's general store – now a block of flats – on the right, looking along the road. Beside it was a hairdressers', and at the end of the next terrace of houses, which still stands, was Fred Johns' fish and chip shop (now a Chinese takeaway). Next door lived a villager who would "lay out the dead" when needed.'

Mr Norris, of Priory Road, Lower Compton, also attended the village school, which, he recalled, sometimes had to use the Methodist church hall at the top of Revel Road for two of its classes.

'Hawkes the butcher operated alongside the Co-op, now a storeroom. A market garden stood on the slope now occupied by town houses. My grandfather Moss was the cellarman at the social club nearby. Everyone knew each other. Many were related and there was a close-knit community atmosphere and spirit,' added Mr Norris, echoing a theme alluded to by many contributors to these articles.

~ A SCHOOL TEACHER'S REMINISCENCES ~

Mary Leigh was headmistress at the little Church of England school in Compton Gifford from 1936 to 1947. She remembered that some children came to school, from the brand-new Efford estate, with 'extremely scanty clothing'. Their parents either had no money or didn't care.

'I loved those dirty little children. I always chose to spend prime time with poorer children; they were often more responsive than the others. Some of the better-off children, you see, had everything and didn't feel any need.'

Headmistress or not, Mary Leigh would often whip out a comb to take lice out of the pupils' hair. 'I obtained their boots through a charity which punched holes into the uppers so that their parents wouldn't sell them at a pawn shop. Times were desperate for some, and the very real, grinding poverty was unbelievable.'

Similar experiences were repeated at other schools during Miss Leigh's thirty years as a headmistress. She even found herself becoming a 'surrogate' mother. At the old Public Central in Cobourg Street, where she taught French from 1927, the father of one pupil of thirteen asked her if she would virtually 'take over' as mother since the child's own had just died. 'I did so, of course, without hesitation. Here was a need I knew I could meet and it was an urgent one. She asked me to help over a wide range of matters, from housekeeping to how to darn her brother's woolly socks. That girl is a great-grandmother now, and she still writes to me!'

She was not the only one to do so. Many former pupils kept in touch with their much-loved headmistress. A number are now in their sixties and a few over seventy. But how did such remarkable long-term correspondence evolve?

'I got to know the girls and – well, I just enjoyed being with them, I suppose,' explained Miss Leigh. 'I saw many of them out of school hours and helped them, say, to learn to swim. As a result, Public won most of the swimming trophies going in Devon during 1934/35, with 90 per cent of the school able to swim. How's that?'

Not that this gracious lady, in her eighty-eighth year when the *Herald* interviewed her, was a pushover for anyone. 'No indeed – I was a strong believer in firm discipline and, believe me, the pupils were happy and secure as a result. Most just obeyed instructions and that was it.' She felt that this was one reason why the Compton school, one of the most popular Plymouth has known, increased its roll from 82 pupils when she took over to more than 300 when she left in 1947.

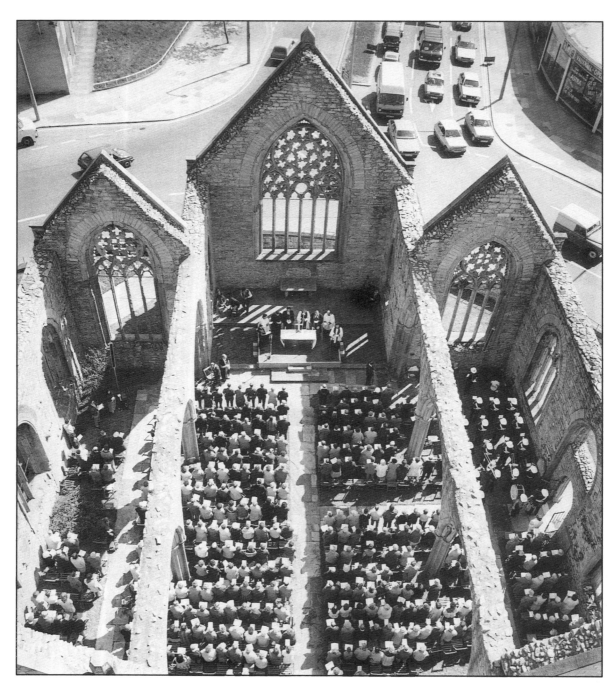

A commemorative
service in Charles
Church

From there she went to Laira Primary, as headmistress, and later filled
the same role at Camel's Head, until her retirement in 1965. Not one easily
to criticise the present generation, she did however emphasise how willing,

A scene in George Street, near Derry's Clock, familiar to Mary Leigh when she was a young child. The former Theatre Royal stood opposite the *Western Morning News* building.

even anxious, most pupils were to learn in the 1930s, 'and the poorer they were, the more that seemed to be the case'.

Although Miss Leigh revelled in her many years as a teacher, another subject close to her heart was Charles Church. She had mixed feelings about the charred remains of that once thriving church squatting forlornly in the middle of a busy roundabout. 'It grieves my heart to see it as it is, given that I remember its former glories. I'm sorry, too, that the historic purpose-built Household of Faith Sunday School, the first in Plymouth, was torn down. I just don't know what to think about the church remaining as it is, a memorial to the Blitz victims.'

Miss Leigh was sure what she felt about the church itself, completed in 1657. 'It was lovely. Here was great enthusiasm, for it had been built on a fine foundation spiritually, its first vicar, Robert Hawker, having ministered there for years. He set the tone with fine, keen Protestant preaching which assured full congregations. The vaulted ceiling was beautiful, and I still have a few pieces of the glorious stained-glass windows. To me the church was particularly wonderful because it was there I got to know God.'

She pointed out that Charles Church became the 'mother' to eight others and cut out large slices of its parish to do so. And she delighted in saying that she went there before she was born, in 1903!

'Yes, my father had been a member for years. He went to the opening of St Jude's and placed coins under its foundation stone. Charles Church was my life. I was secretary during the war and ran the Sisterhoods for forty-five years, as well as a girls' Bible class. When it was blitzed in 1941 it was one of the few things that made me cry. My life seemed to be completely broken on that day.'

But Mary Leigh is still radiant at 91, although visually handicapped. She said that she now attended St Matthias Church, North Hill, as did the two other known survivors of the old Charles Church. It is plain that much of the old spirit from that church lived on within her, and many people were the beneficiaries.

~ SHOPS AND PUBS IN DEVONPORT ~

Gerald Barker, who has compiled seven pictorial histories of old Devonport, easily identified William Street, as it was in the early 1900s. It was the principal thoroughfare in Morice Town.

'On the right-hand side, above the awning, were three brass balls denoting one of the numerous pawnbrokers' shops that once existed in Devonport. The three trees on the left-hand side were part of Sparrow Park that at one time provided a pleasant oasis at the bottom of Albert Road, adjacent to the Albert Gate of HM Dockyard.

'In 1910 the Morice Town Picture House was built, standing in the vicinity of the lamp-post on the opposite side of the road to the Free House, seen in the picture. In 1933 it was gutted by a disastrous fire that broke out at midday, just before the opening of the children's matinee.'

Mr Barker, of Burnham Park Road, Peverell, and something of a walking text-book on old Devonport, recalled that double tram-lines were laid in 1910. He said that at one time William Street had twelve public houses, four eating-houses and three workmen's dining rooms – all of which 'must have produced an unforgettable atmosphere'.

William Street, in Morice Town, in the early 1900s

52

St Levan Road, with its well-known railway bridge

Mr George Light was born in William Street and lived there until 1933. He remembered that in those days it was known as 'little Jerusalem' by servicemen because of its five naval outfitters – Greenburgh, Erlich, Caplan, Lake and Bloom. A director of Plymouth Argyle, Peter Bloom, is a descendant of the last-named.

Mr Light, of Woodford Crescent, Plympton, recalled that there were seven pubs: the Silver Tree, the Steam Reserve, the Prince Arthur – which overlooked Sparrow Park – the Wellington, the Royal Alfred, the Royal Standard and the Morice Town wine and spirit vaults. He said that his grandfather, who was a master baker, had a popular restaurant at 26 William Street from 1908 to 1921. 'He was then steward of an RAOB club at those premises until 1933, when we moved to Charlotte Street.'

William Street was heavily bombed during the 1941 Blitz and what remained was incorporated into the Dockyard's extension after the war.

Mr R. Murray lived at 33 St Levan Road and remembered many of the shops seen in the second photograph.

'The first shop on the right was Albert and Jean Brimacombe's, better known as "Weevils". There were four more shops on the same side, towards the railway bridge. These were Pellings the tobacconists, Bewals confectioners, a butcher's shop owned by Bill Davis, and Gregory. Opposite was a cobblers' shop and, past the bridge, Darkie Venning's St Levan's Inn – he himself was a former LSWR fireman.'

~ PANTOMIME AT THE GRAND THEATRE ~

The old Grand Theatre in Union Street boasted the largest stage west of Bristol. Many readers had happy memories of visits to the Grand, not least when the legendary Randolph Sutton topped the bill.

Mr L. Weeks of Terra Nova Green, Milehouse, recalled that he went there often as a child. The great attraction during the 1920s was the annual pantomime when, on one occasion, he saw Randolph Sutton introduce his great hit song 'On Mother Riley's Doorstep'.

'We queued early on each Boxing Day afternoon at the gallery entrance, waiting to rush up the steep stairs to claim front seats. My family lived next door to the Robin Hood Inn, where a very young Donald Peers lodged during his first pantomime appearance, in 1929.'

L. Boon of Ince Close, Torpoint, was another reader who remembered seeing Randolph Sutton. The entertainer appeared on stage in costumes glittering with spangles and sequins, and sang cheeky songs. 'The young "flappers" were stage-struck and able to buy a souvenir postcard for 1d.'

This reader also recalled a shop further along Union Street which sold Teddy Weeks' cough drops at a penny a packet. 'You could look through the window and see the mixture being stretched and pulled like dough, before being made into a lozenge mixture of peppermint, aniseed, cloves, etc. Then there was May's Dairy, with its marble-top tables, where you could buy junket and clotted cream for 2d. a portion.'

The Stonehouse end of Union Street before the First World War; the Grand Theatre was showing *The Girl Who Lost Her Character*.

A street scene outside
the Grand theatre
c.1880

Mrs Maud Callow remembered walking to the Grand with her family, from Monument Hill, Devonport, more than seventy-five years ago. One production she clearly remembered was *High Heels and Silk Stockings*, when her sister-in-law was in the chorus.

Mrs B.M. Clifton was another reader who went to the theatre as a small girl, and who did errands for neighbours in order to earn the 3d. it cost to get into 'the gods'. She cried after twice seeing a very sad play called *East Lynn* , and she was not the only one. 'People would leave the theatre crying, even the men had red eyes. There were also other plays like *Murder in the Red Barn*, which was the talk of the town, *The Iron Mask* and *The Face at the Window*.'

Later the Grand Theatre was turned into a cinema, then after the last war it was used as a site for pram making.

Mr R.C. Fuzzard of Goonrea, West Looe, remembered some of the other properties near the theatre. These included: Stanbury's the toy shop; Darch's dining-rooms; Graspan House – home of the much-respected Dr W.H. Waterfield – and, next to it, King Fields shop which sold medals and uniforms. The naval tailor Bendon was next, followed by Wakeling's the photographers, a furniture shop owned by a Mr Lazarus, and then Timothy White's the chemist.

~ TELEGRAMS AND NEW YEAR REVELRIES ~

Vic Saundercock, author of the book *Plymouth: Yesterday, Today*, had many reminiscences of the old post office featured in the photograph. He said that it was also the savings bank, telegraph office and government annuity and money order office, and that some departments never closed. All you had to do to send a telegram at any hour was to go to the side entrance,

where you would receive service. Business hours were from 8 a.m. to 8
p.m. on weekdays, with Sunday opening between 9 and 10.30 a.m. The
telegraph business was open twenty-four hours, and collection of letters
took place between 5 a.m. and 8.45 p.m.

Another reader had memories of the adjoining Guildhall Square on New
Year's Eve. He recalled one occasion when two sailors climbed on to the
post office roof and couldn't get off again; eventually they gave themselves
up to the Navy patrol.

Many people remembered carol singing around the Christmas tree in
Guildhall Square, as well as hearty community singing to welcome in the
New Year.

Mr Fuzzard, writing in his late eighties, remembered Churchill's fish
shop along Westwell Street, near the Square. This was next door to
Westwell Gardens which at one time was a cemetery. He said that when it
was made into a garden, the headstones were placed around the walls and
the bones that were uncovered were taken elsewhere. Blundells brewery
was opposite the gardens.

~ THE RAILWAY IN PLYMOUTH ~

Friary Station was the terminus of the old Southern Railway and well
known to many Plymothians. Stan Quick of North Road West had more
reason than most to remember it – he lived at 2 Friary Street in his early
years and enjoyed riding in the old steam trains.

He recalled that the trip to Turnchapel cost 2d. 'We would then walk to
Jennycliff and, after a day there, return in the evening to Friary.

Friary Station, a busy railway terminus in the early 1930s

'Many of the circus shows in those days unloaded all their animals at Friary and would then parade through the town. When we were small we all used to play behind the boardings at the rear of Smith's paper shop, near the station.'

R.J. Ward of Downfield Drive, Plympton, suggested that the train seen leaving was probably bound for Waterloo, via Bere Alston, Tavistock, Okehampton and Exeter, a run that was known as the Atlantic Coast Express. He also thought that the smaller train on the right was what was known locally as the Turnchapel Express, which ran to Lucas Terrace Halt, Plymstock, Oreston and Turnchapel at 3d. return, with half fare for children.

'As a young lad I can remember soldiers arriving at Friary Station en route to Mutley and Crownhill Barracks, with horses and bands. The fish which was landed at the Barbican was boxed and iced and then taken to Friary Station by horse and cart. There was an entrance to the station for this traffic from Exeter Street, opposite the Burton Boys pub, through iron gates.'

~ KING'S ROAD STATION ~

Edna Nation of Hastings Terrace remembered the old station very well: as a child she lived opposite it, in Paradise Road. She said that the old gas-lit station was then a very busy place because although wages were low nearly everyone could afford to travel by rail. Many Dockyardies used King's Road and fresh farm produce arrived there for the popular Devonport market, with horses and wagons waiting at the entrance to deliver it.

The old King's Road railway station in Devonport; the site is now occupied by the College of Further Education

Mrs Nation recalled that the waiting room had a coal fire and upholstered seats. 'Although everyone had access there was no vandalism because we were disciplined at home and in our schools. Outside, waiting for passengers, were horse-drawn carriages with cabbies on top in hat and tails. Some children would jump on the axle for a ride up the hill, until others shouted "whip behind" so that the cabbie would swish back his long whip and they would soon jump off!'

Mrs Nation remembered tea parties from the nearby Stoke Damerel Church when parents, children and neighbours filled the platform on a day out to Bere Ferrers or Bere Alston, 'which seemed miles away'.

Decades ago, when the Edgcumbe family used the train, the station's dining-room was opened and a meal prepared just in case it was needed, a correspondent from Admiralty Street observed. 'The staff all lined up to greet them,' she added. Her memories go a long way back to the time when the road outside the station was being made up and the workers wore bowler hats as they toiled away!

As another correspondent pointed out, King's Road could be confused with Friary Station because both had Gothic arches. Eventually the old original part of the station – at the far end in the picture – was sealed off and leased to the Devonport Mineral Water Company.

✿ ✿ ✿

~ GUNNERSIDE SCHOOL ~

This photograph struck an emotional chord in a number of people's hearts, all of whom remembered that the school was run by three remarkable sisters, though the buildings did lack certain basic facilities.

Mrs Jeanne Curle still has her kindergarten school reports from Gunnerside, where she made three especially good friends in Molly Lake and Myrtle and Betty Bray. They all moved on to finish their education at Smeaton College in Citadel Road. 'Another pupil, Margaret Gunn, herself became a headmistress and taught my children.'

Mrs Curle, whose maiden name was Mason, recalled that Gunnerside was owned by the Misses Hilda, Bertha and Phoebe Stranger, and that it was housed in two large buildings. The school colours were gold and blue stripes. 'As it had no gym of its own, we had to form into a "crocodile" and walk to a hall off Houndiscombe Road.'

When the school finally closed, said Mrs Curle, the Stranger sisters moved further up the road to live in another of the large houses, which is now occupied by her doctor's surgery.

Another former pupil was Mrs Pat Kingdon, who was there from 1927 until 1935. The school, she said, was established in 1860; half of it was on one side of the entrance to Evelyn Place and half was on the other side.

Gunnerside School, in Torrington Place, recalled with affection by its former pupils

'When we had a science lesson we had to walk along Evelyn Place to St Lawrence Road as the laboratory was in St Lawrence Yard over a builder's premises. We used to attend lessons between 9 a.m. and 1 p.m. weekdays, but stopped at 12 noon on Saturdays. We had quite a bit of homework to keep us busy and, of course, there was sport in the afternoon.'

Mrs Kingdon was a day pupil, although Gunnerside also took boarders, boys as well as girls. During her time there one of the teachers was Margery Walling, daughter of A.J. Walling, a distinguished West Country journalist at that time editing the old *Western Independent*. He wrote many books, including a classic, *The Story of Plymouth*.

Interestingly, two other schools were near Gunnerside – Plymouth High School for Girls, at the top of St Lawrence Road, and Headland College for Girls, in North Hill.

When the school closed, the building became an old people's home, observed Mr Steve Dey, secretary of the Plymouth Guild of Community Service. Digging into the archives, he discovered that the Guild ran the home there from 1941 until 1958, when it closed. The Guild's annual report for 1942/43 says that the home 'has already created its own place in the affections of Plymouth'.

It continued: 'Here we have three houses – converted, redecorated and equipped – where old people live as guests, and in no sense dwell in an "institution". The residents, who are mostly supplementary pensioners, are enabled by the Assistance Board to meet the entire cost of their board and lodging, and there is therefore a complete absence of patronage. The old people themselves are their own advertisement, and it is a privilege to serve them.'

The 1957 annual report, after pointing out that the city's elderly were being cared for 'on a scale that is rarely equalled in any other part of the country', records that with the closure 'ends our pioneer effort to establish a small residential home'.

~ THE HOE GRAMMAR SCHOOL ~

Former Lord Mayor W. Ivor Thompson had vivid memories of this well-known school. He was one of a clutch of councillors educated at the school; others included Leslie F. Paul, Percy Pascoe, Frank Chapman, John Pascoe and Ron King. But it was to the legendary G.P. Dymond, headmaster for over fifty years, that Mr Thompson drew attention; he, too, was a former Lord Mayor.

The Hoe Grammar School was established in 1867 and Mr Dymond became its principal twenty years later. He graduated from London University in 1891 and obtained his MA in English in 1903. He celebrated this by hiring a steam ferry boat and taking the entire school to Calstock, where they enjoyed a strawberry tea.

The Hoe Grammar School before the Blitz in 1941

It seems that Mr Dymond proved equally at home whether teaching Greek, Latin, modern languages, science or maths. He enjoyed every moment and nothing gave him greater pleasure than seeing some backward child making slow but steady progress. He could make the dullest subject live and many remember the humorous asides that lit up his lessons.

He also enjoyed intellectual stimulus outside his school life 'by reading good books, hearing good lectures and joining literary societies'.

The Duke and Duchess of York, later King George VI and Queen Elizabeth, opening the new Orthopaedic Hospital at Mount Gould in 1932; on their left are Bert Medland, a city councillor and future Labour MP for Plymouth Drake, and G.P. Dymond, the Lord Mayor of the time and headmaster of Hoe Grammar for over fifty years.

The school was blitzed in March 1941 and closed the following month. The Old Drakonian Association of ex-pupils flourished through many decades, although inevitably by now it is only a shadow of its former self.

Mr J.A. Carroll of Crossway, Plympton, noted that the site of the old grammar school is now occupied by the YWCA.

~ *JUNKET AND CREAM FOR 1s. 6d.* ~

Readers who worked in the old Westwell Street – in one case as long ago as 1915 – were quick to supply details of the scene in this photograph.

Mr Frank Thomas of Western Drive, Laira, had many memories of the street: he worked there when he was a lad in 1915 as an errand boy for Mr Joel Roberts, who ran a florist and vegetable shop just about opposite where the tramcar is seen. 'I used to take supplies to Millbay Docks for the troops then stationed on Drake's Island, as well as to various hotels and houses around town.'

Mr Thomas recalled that the trams used to turn off into Basket Street en route to St Andrew's Cross and Spooners' corner, and thence into Old Town Street.

The picture had a similar effect on Mrs Maisie Woolley of Venn Grove, Hartley, who said it 'jerked my heart'. The reason for this is the Blundells dray standing outside the same firm in which her father worked until it was blitzed. 'I well remember a dairy on the opposite side of the street where one could buy a dish of junket and cream for about 1s. 6d., and very delicious it was too!'

Mr S. Robertson correctly picked out the Guildhall on the right, with Bedford Street in the distance, and the GPO almost in front of the tram. He also pointed out that the tree in the foreground is now outside the municipal offices and that one of the two trees on either side of the Guildhall still stands. That part of Bedford Street visible in the picture is now occupied by Dingles.

More of the shops were identified by Des Leach of Hill Crest, Mannamead. These included, on the right: Perkin Bros. the outfitters, on the corner of Basket Street; Davis Keelers the opticians; Lords; Shands; and the Embankment Coach Company. He also remembered, on the other side: Tremaynes the second-hand bookshop; Churchill's the fishmongers; Pryor's Academy; The Three Towns Dairy and Battershill's the newsagent.

Mr Jack Hallett observed that the tramcar was a Wilton 48-seater with an open top. His father was a senior motorman and subsequently an inspector of Plymouth Tramways. 'On several occasions he drove the trams with the future kings Edward VIII and George VI as passengers; that was when they were midshipmen stationed at the Royal Naval Barracks. In those days they had no police protection.'

Mr Hallett said that the shop in the centre at the top of the picture, in Bedford Street, was John Yeo's, the department store that was eventually swallowed up by the Debenham chain. There is some disagreement about this, however, since other readers claimed that it was Pophams.

A view of Westwell Street, which led on to Bedford Street, taken before the Second World War

George Street Baptist
Church after the Blitz

Mrs Betty Chandler remembered going to a gym class every Monday
evening at George Street Baptist Church hall, also seen in the picture. This
was supervised by silver-haired Mrs Scantlebury, dressed in a short maroon
gymslip and a cream blouse.

'The pianist played us in to 'An English Country Garden', the signature tune. We marched in a long line down the hall, divided, came down in twos and then fours, spaced out and exercised. It was all a great joy! When our hour was over the older girls began with a grand march and exercising with wooden clubs, while we "tinies" swung dumbells.'

Sunday evening services at George Street Baptist Church were so packed that the congregation started queuing at 4.30 p.m., recalled Mr James Whearn of Widey View, Hartley.

'It was a little like queuing for the cinema or the "gods" at one of the theatres. The attraction was of a very different kind, though – a powerful figure by the name of J. Wilkinson Riddle, who preached with rare power and eloquence, holding his vast congregation, easily, for up to 45 minutes. He was a profound man, whose exposition of the scriptures on a systematic basis was very different from much of what now passes for preaching.'

Mr Wilkinson Riddle had a distinguished ministry in Baptist churches and his contribution to Plymouth's Christian life was immense. Mr Whearn maintained that the city has never known such a preacher since. Riddle was always willing to challenge his congregations in direct and vigorous terms – 'perhaps that was one secret of his great success'.

~ SHOPPING FOR BROKEN BISCUITS ~

Typical Plymouth weather! Streets glisten with rain beneath a grey sky and pedestrians scurry past to avoid the downpour. Many of the city streets were once paved with stone 'setts' like those shown in the picture on the following page. These granite blocks provided a hardwearing and attractive road surface but gave a bumpy and dangerous ride for unwary cyclists. In the background the road is closed to traffic as yet another bomb site is cleared for redevelopment.

The old shops with clapboard frontages, complete with advertisements, stirred the memories of a number of *Herald* readers, many of whom correctly identified the scene as being at the junction of Russell Street and Morley Street, with Willow Street on the right.

Mr Giles, now of Laira, was born in Willow Plot, at the top of which was Vosper's radio shop, the forerunner of Vosper's motors. At the end of the row shown here, on the left hand side, was Russell's store whose motto was 'Where Less Buys More'.

Trevors, the newsagents, is seen on the left of the picture which was taken in the 1950s. Eric Dixon remembered visiting the newsagents for his weekly copy of *Wizard* and *Hotspur* comics. 'My parents kept a dairy and general store further along Russell Street,' he wrote. 'I recall workmen coming in from the brass foundry in Mill Street with their bottles for a penny's worth of milk for their tea.

At the junction of
Russell Street and
Morley Street.

Mrs Sarah Butler pointed out that the new Cornwall Street was being laid at the time the picture was taken. She identifies Walkers, the chemist, and J.R. Adams, the tobacconist and confectioners, where, as a young girl, she went to work in 1955. 'Within a few days I met my husband, Reg, who was born and bred in Morley Street. We have now been happily married for over 35 years.'

Mrs Stella Tucker of Knowle Avenue said she remembered walking through the area during an air raid with her future husband when most of its shops were alight. 'My husband remembers that the firemen's pumps were out of action so fire just spread from one shop to another.

Some of the shops on the right bear the scars of wartime damage with flaking plaster and smoke stained walls. Much of Plymouth survived in this careworn fashion in the decade following the war, small businesses continuing to occupy premises that had sustained considerable damage, with upper storeys uninhabitable.

As the new Plymouth emerged from the ashes of the old city, many smaller shops simply disappeared as people began to shop in the bigger stores in the newly built city centre.

The early years of the 1950s were the time of utility furniture, with some goods, including petrol, remaining on ration, and with cars being out of the reach of most families. The motorcycle and sidecar, seen in the centre of the photograph, was a popular mode of family transport, with two passengers on the bike at the mercy of the elements, and two in the sidecar along with the luggage! Stephen Woods of Plymstock recalled family holidays to Cornwall on his father's motorbike and sidecar. 'It was an ex Army BSA 500cc bike that was always difficult to start. But it took us many a mile out into the countryside.'

Despite this austerity, or perhaps because of it, people endured the grey days of post-war Britain and most memories of the time recall the feeling of optimism for the future. The rebuilding of the city provided many jobs for those recently returned from the war, while goods and provisions began to reappear in the shops.

Even so sweet rationing continued into the early fifties and, for children, chocolate was a luxury to be savoured. Jeanne Curle of Honiton Close recalled that you could buy bags of broken biscuits at Russells. 'The unbroken biscuits were displayed in large tins with glass lids so you could see which kind they were. I used to love going in there with my mother as I was always allowed to pick out the ones I liked best, usually the chocolate variety.

~ CHURCH BELLS IN WHIMPLE STREET ~

The good old days? Don't try telling that to Fred Matthews of Plympton; he has seen the other side. 'No internal plumbing whatever; every drop of fresh water carried up to our top flat from a tap in the back yard, with every drop of dirty water carried back down.' That was Whimple Street over 75 years ago, when Mr Matthews lived there.

From No. 3 the family moved to No. 4 and things changed for the better. 'That was luxury indeed. We had electric light and a stone kitchen sink with a cold water tap – what more could we want?'

Mr Matthews, of Underlane, remembered that when female telephone operators arrived either late for work or for weekend duties they rang a concealed bell at the entrance to the exchange. A key was lowered down to them on a line from the top floor. This was then dutifully pulled back up after the operator had closed the entrance door.

He also recalled that a 'dear old Italian chap with a wooden leg could be seen at the top end of Whimple Street with his handcart which had been manhandled by us kids from Palace Street. In the summer he sold ice-cream and in winter roast chestnuts.'

Mrs Jeanne Curle pointed out that the picture also showed part of St Andrew's Church, the old municipal offices and the law courts, Basket and Bedford Streets and Bateman's Corner with its huge model of a pair of

The city centre in the early 1940s, taken from a window of the telephone exchange at the corner of Whimple and Kinterbury Streets

spectacles on the frontage. She noted that although the old memorial at the front of St Andrew's was damaged in the Blitz, the two statues survived and were relocated at the new Guildhall.

Mrs Gladys Williams of Kingsbridge said that there was a little garden with two seats near the memorial, 'and the bedding plants were nearly always geraniums. I sat there many times listening to the church bells which on the hour rang out a tune, sometimes a well-known hymn or a song. People used to stand still just to listen – lovely, peaceful and happy days they were!'

~ ROAD WORKS IN BEDFORD STREET ~

Many people had memories of working in shops in Bedford Street during the 1930s. Robert Cross of Warwick Orchard Close, for instance, was an assistant in Hepworth's – clearly seen on the corner – in 1933-34. He remembered that the shop on the right of that store was Etam.

Someone else with personal memories was George Wetherell, who pointed out that the workmen are removing a 'No entry' sign to make way for traffic lights.

'The view is right up Bedford Street to Spooners' corner, showing part of the island site, the removal of which the City Fathers debated about for ten years – and Hitler did the job in one night.' The roads were surfaced with wooden blocks, he added, 'and what a slippery nuisance they were on a wet day for pedestrians and motorists. Further up the street, below the shop blind, is the boiler which sealed the blocks with molten tar.'

Mr Wetherall, of Stoggy Lane, Plympton, noted that the beautiful arched doorway further up, showing a small wall sign, belonged to the Road Transport and General Insurance Co. Ltd, while the floor above was occupied by accountant Gerald Whitmarsh. 'He was a Liberal parliamentary candidate and that's where he started Western Credit Services. He was also chairman of Devon County Council.'

The corner of Bedford Street and George Street on a busy winter's day in the 1930s

~ MILLBAY STATION ~

Not a great many people recognised Millbay Station in the picture on the following page, though it survived for some time after the last war. George Wetherell, however, remembered it well because he arrived there after a 14 hour train journey from Newcastle in May 1931.

'I landed at the station at 5 a.m. It was the dirtiest, coldest one I had ever been in. The few night employees didn't seem to care – they were more interested in getting home or back into "kip". I was directed to Plymouth Hoe. The morning sun was just coming through, visibility was excellent, the Sound was a millpond, the trees in full leaf and the beds full of flowers. It was the loveliest sight I had ever seen; I was transfixed and converted. I soon became a keener Plymothian than many of the locals!'

Mr Patrick McLaughlin reported to stationmaster Arthur Prior on 1 May 1939, before starting his job in the booking office. 'We used to have our morning cuppa in the refreshment rooms, often served by Maisie Sticks or one of the McCarthy sisters – it was certainly service with a smile in those days!'

Mr McLaughlin, of Conrad Road, Manadon, recalled that the most popular excursions in those pre-war days were trips to the moor, especially on a Sunday when the fare was sixpence ha'penny return for a half day. Evening trips were often run to St Ives and Newquay.

Looking back on those days, Mr Ted Hocking of Plympton said that if he was lucky arriving at Millbay Station by train sometimes coincided with the berthing of GWR tenders carrying passengers from an ocean liner anchored in the Sound. K. Browning of Valletort Road remembered travelling as a child, in the 1930s, from Millbay to Bristol Temple Meads at a cost of 5s. return.

The former Millbay Station, the site of which is now occupied by Plymouth Pavilions

Mr Philip Powell of Dunstone View, Plymstock, observed that Millbay had very large decorative entrance posts. He said that a tank and gun from the First World War used to stand on plinths near the trees of the adjoining Millbay Park. Beyond were the remains of the Ballard Institute, of which he was a member. 'It was a wonderful place for boys,' he recalled.

Referring to Millbay Park, Mr S. Robertson pointed out that hundreds of soldiers rested there on their return from Dunkirk.

SIXPENNY TRAIN TRIPS ON THE 'WOOLWORTH SPECIAL'

Mutley railway station was served by most of the mainline trains which started at Millbay terminus. What most readers remembered, however, were the sixpenny rides to neighbouring beauty spots.

The small station was a constant source of delight to Mrs A.I. Luff when she was a child in the 1920s. 'Our Sunday School outings from Peverell Park Methodist Church started from there, the destination being either Bere Alston or Cornwood. The journey was a sheer delight – I think we imagined we were going halfway round the world!'

Mrs Luff, of Woodland Drive, Merafield, remembered the little slot machines on the platform where a bar of Nestlés chocolate could be bought for 1d. She said that on summer Sunday afternoons, at 4.30 precisely, a train left Mutley for Shaugh Bridge, Clearbrook and Yelverton, and the

The houses and the church remain, but Mutley railway station has long since disappeared.

ticket cost 6d. 'This train was referred to as the Woolworth train because the ticket never cost more than 6d. They were truly magical days.'

There was a slope leading down to the platform, recalled A. R. Bennet of Chaddlewood Avenue. 'A cab rank stood at the top of this slope, with a hut for the cabbie. I even remember the names of the two cab drivers – one was a Mr Cole and the other was George Chaff, who lived in Clifton Street.'

Bertram LeBearn of Wolseley Road said that Mutley was the station for the 'toffs', the residents of Mannamead and Hartley. 'I was taken by my parents, practically every Saturday, to catch the 2.13 p.m. to Shaugh or Yelverton, or the 2.30 p.m. to Cornwood or Ivybridge for an afternoon in the country or on the moors. The trains were normally busy enough to have about six coaches, non-corridor, hauled by a tank engine.

'The "motor" trains of one to four saloon coaches provided a regular service between Plympton and Saltash for "Yardies" and other workmen and, later in the day, for shoppers. In those times the railways under private ownership could run to time at a profit. They were litter-free and as clean as coal-powered locomotives would allow.'

Bill Canter from Penzance remembered the nearby Mutley Baptist Church, shown in the picture, because he was sent home from its Sunday School for fooling around! He also recalled the Mutley Assembly Rooms, with an L-shaped dance floor.

PRE-WAR UNION STREET AND DEVONPORT'S BUSY MARKET

The bleak reminder of the old Devonport market is probably among the most evocative of Plymouth's pre-war relics. Many people would like to see it restored to its rightful owners, instead of squatting sadly inside the Dockyard wall, looking like a cast-off orphan.

Mr David Coleman was one of many people who remembered the market. An old Devonport boy, he spent weekends with the Viggers farming family at Bere Alston during the Blitz. The connection is that they were regulars at the old Devonport market which was 'a hive of activity on Saturdays, with farmers from all around Plymouth selling their produce'.

Mr Coleman, of Crabtree Villas, Plymouth Road, recalled that the adjacent Cumberland Street was a very busy shopping thoroughfare leading to the bottom of Fore Street. Just across from the market, behind the clock tower, was a 'slaughter-house', and in an opening just off Cumberland Street a rag-and-bone store 'where we could sell rabbit skins for sixpence and jamjars two for a ha'penny. Happy days! We were poor but honest and did enjoy life.'

The gaunt remains
of Devonport's once-
bustling market

Miss Kim Palmer noted that the market was built in 1852 and that the building on the left-hand corner was York Street School, where her mother, then Sylvia Wood, went as a child. So did Len Harvey, the famous boxer. Miss Palmer, of Park Avenue, Devonport, pointed out that the road

An aerial view of Union Street and its surroundings, taken before the Second World War

between the market and the school was called Market Street, where the Post Office Inn could be found, and led to Chapel Street and St Aubyn's Church.

Mr Norman Peter lived at 24A Barrack Street, off Market Square, 'which was really more of a triangle'. 'As a member of the Air Defence Corps, I was stationed as a cycle messenger in the control centre that was under the corner of the market.' He said that his parents were the last people to leave the area during the post-war Dockyard extension, and by that time the new wall ran almost the whole length of Chapel Street.

The above photograph, showing pre-war Union Street, elicited many memories from people who either lived or worked there. Mr Albert Taylor of Moorland View, Derriford, estimated that the picture was taken about 1,500 feet above the North Quay inner basin in Millbay Docks, and before the building of the Regent and Gaumont cinemas.

Working clockwise, he named Tracey, Well, Flora, Henry, Courtenay and Frankfort Streets, leading into Union Street, with its railway arch carrying the old GWR line to North Road Station. Then comes The Octagon, Bath Street, Millbay Station and, at the base, Sawrey and Moir Streets. The streets on the left-hand side are mainly still there, though with altered lines – Phoenix, Rendle, Octagon, King and Harwell Streets among them.

David Coleman said that the large store seen in The Octagon was Jay's the furnishers, which burned spectacularly during the Blitz. The Palace

Theatre is clearly visible and he remembered seeing Max Miller, Jessie Matthews and Phyllis Dixie – among other artists – perform there.

Mr S. Robertson was able to pick out the house in which he was born, next to what was Jacob's (now Knights' warehouse) in King Street.

~ *VINTAGE DEVONPORT* ~

Catherine Street ran parallel to St Aubyn and Chapel Streets and led into Fore Street in the heart of old Devonport. At its end, on the left-hand side, stood the huge pile of the Royal Sailors' Rest, or 'Aggie Weston's', erected in 1879 thanks to the foresight of the redoubtable Dame Agnes Weston and her companion, Sophia Wintz.

Gerald Barker – recalled that a performer, such as a conjuror, would entertain passers-by on the opposite side to the Sailors' Rest.

At the bottom of the hill, and on the other side of the street, stood Jimmy Love's shop – he was very popular with the people of Devonport. 'The picture clearly shows the clock of this emporium. Flags emblazoned with the lettering "J. B. Love" sometimes flew from the top of the tall beautiful roofs that were all done in Victorian wrought-iron style. The building was huge and usually thronged with customers. It was on a par with Jimmy Tozer's and Boold's shops.'

Mr Barker also remembered that at Christmas time, Love's shop and the surrounding streets became a fairyland, lit by straggling electrical wires. This magnificent building, spreading around the corner along Willis Street towards old Edinburgh Street, by the Dockyard wall, was destroyed in the Blitz of April 1941.

'Just out of view, standing further back along the street from the wall with the advertisements, was one of the gateways leading into Devonport

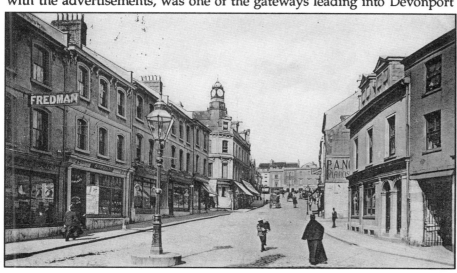

Catherine Street, Devonport, taken in the mid 1920s

75

market. Parades would sometimes march down the hill, passing the conjuror's "spot" and the garage where a skinny boy called Len Harvey worked; he was later to become the world light-heavyweight boxing champion,' added Mr Barker.

'Three doors down the marchers would pass "Old Daddy's pawn shop". Ike Rogers was a fatherly figure to many as they lined up outside his shop on Monday mornings. He was the life-saver for many a poor Devonport family, some of whom would pawn their possessions on Mondays and get them out again on Fridays.'

~ *DIVING OFF THE OLD PIER* ~

The old pier still conjures up memories of happy days spent listening to the band, dancing on the ballroom floor, playing the machines or diving into the Sound from one of its many boards.

The Sunday concerts were remembered by Mrs Enid Ware: 'There were various steamer trips that left from the pier, but what most of us loved were the dances. I was a VAD nurse at the Naval Hospital during the war and was asked to take a few of the Yorkshire boys on the staff to the pier, and they loved it. There was also a swimming club and an angling group – so much activity and none of it cost more than a shilling.'

Mr P.J. Serridge was a member of the Plymouth Adventure Swimming Club based under the pier. He said that people look at him with amazement when he tells them that the Lord Mayor would attend the opening dips in April or May, along with the Plymouth Transport Band.

He also pointed out that the swimming club held its galas in the sea off the pier. 'My father, a well-known diving champion, was the first man to dive off the pier's stage engulfed in flames.'

A much-loved landmark – the old pier, off The Hoe

~ BILLACOMBE ROAD IN QUIETER TIMES ~

This view of Billacombe Road shows a scene very different from today's: the left of the road is now the A379 dual carriageway. Mr Chapman of Broadland Lane, Plymstock, claimed that all the houses except the first one, in the foreground, have been demolished.

'As a member of the defiant Plympton Rural District Council for many years I was privileged to see the area expand from around 8,500 to approximately 28,000 people in three decades. New bungalows, a service station and an industrial site now appear on the north side of the dual carriageway.'

The entrance to Plymstock Station was on the right, where the car is parked, and Mr E.G. Mitchell from Hooe noted that the tall building in the middle distance was a stone crusher, later transferred to the mouth of the creek.

Billacombe Road, looking towards Laira Bridge, taken before it was included within the city boundary

R.C. Perry from Higher Compton pointed out that the Limmer & Trinidad Lake Asphalt Co. depot office is on the left and beyond that the wharf with the loading plant used for loading boats with stone aggregate from the nearby quarry. Beyond that again was the Morley Arms, the Iron Bridge and, in the distance, one of the two power station chimneys, recently pulled down.

'The clock over the door of the asphalt company's office was useful for estimating the chances of getting to work on time. A gap of six inches between the telegraph pole, on the left of the road, and the asphalt depot wall enabled the local constable to stand with his back pressed against the wall and peer through the gap to maintain observation on the halt sign further down the road, without himself being seen. There was usually a good crop of miscreants for his notebook!'

Mrs E. Bojanitz of Wembury travelled along the road every day to and from work. 'One morning my motorcycle's points moved and as I did not have a magneto spanner I called in at a very small garage, where the mill used to be, to buy one. The very young fellow there rudely told me to go and buy one at the garage where I bought my petrol. I had to push the 350 cc motorcycle over to Follands' Garage. I wonder if that uncouth boy stayed long in his employment!'

Former city and county councillor and Lord Mayor W. Ivor Thompson knew the area well because his parents lived at 4 Pomphlett Villas from the mid 1920s until after the war, and he did likewise until his marriage in 1942.

"From about 1925 to 1927, when I was a pupil at Hoe Grammar School, I had to catch a train from Plymstock Station to Friary, from where I would walk to school in Lockyer Street. The passenger platform at Plymstock was on the far – northern – side with no access from the road except across the track. To catch the train I had to walk under the rail bridge, over the road and then up another road to the passenger platform. From our house I could look across the creek and up to the higher ground beyond from where I could see the smoke of the train as it left Oreston Station. I would then have to run to the station to catch the train as it came round.'

~ GRACIOUS LIVING IN A COUNTRY HOUSE ~

The Radford Estate in Higher Hooe (now Radford Park) belonged in turn to the Radford, Bulteel and Harris families. It passed to the latter in about 1480 and the mansion (shown in the photograph) was built in the sixteenth century.

The best-known member of the Harris dynasty was Sir Christopher Harris, an MP for Plymouth during the seventeenth century and a close friend of Drake, Raleigh and Hawkins. Some of the gold and silver blocks

Radford House, Higher Hooe, before it was demolished in the 1930s

which Sir Francis Drake brought back from the South Seas were stored at the house. It is also recorded that Sir Christopher held Sir Walter Raleigh prisoner at Radford on his return to Plymouth in 1618, after an abortive search for gold in Guiana.

During the Civil War silver plate was buried in the grounds and was discovered two hundred years later by a farmer ploughing a field.

Mr Leonard Norsworthy of Amados Drive, Plympton, worked on the estate as a gardener in 1927 with his brother, Jack, who was head gardener there, and was well acquainted with the history of Radford.

More information was supplied by the late Mrs Vera Lambert whose father used to work on the estate, looking after the cattle. She said that the family lived in the armoury building, which still stands. Mrs Lambert recalled the Adam ceilings in most of the fifty rooms in Radford House, the seventeenth-century staircase, the rich oak panelling of the dining-hall and the stables to the east of the building. She remembered too the titled people who arrived by pony and trap for parties, when the house used to throb with a gay social life.

Radford House was bought by 'Billy' Mitchell just before the First World War and troops were billeted there during that conflict. The old place was pulled down in 1937, but Mrs Lambert felt that this need not have happened since all it needed was a new roof; it could have been put to good use as a country folk museum or even a residential home but, alas, went the way of so many of Plymouth's old mansions.

~ STONEHOUSE HALL ~

This impressive building was once the centre of local government in Stonehouse until it became redundant in 1914 when Stonehouse and

Stonehouse Town
Hall, at one time a hub
of local government
before the
amalgamation of
the three towns; in
the foreground is
a policeman.

Devonport were amalgamated with Plymouth at the instigation of the Admiralty, who wanted to deal with one authority, instead of three, in the event of war.

Pamela Cane, who used to live in nearby George Place, recalled that part of the building was an ante-natal and baby clinic; she used to take her daughter, Irene, there each week for her weighing, injections and medical check-ups. 'The entrance faced Emma Place, another great street of beautiful houses. It was a lovely old building. Mrs Baskerville was the caretaker and cleaner and she gave me sixpence pocket money each week if I cleaned my shoes – she was a great believer in cleanliness.'

Mr T. Taylor of Albion Court, Torpoint, said that his mother used to attend the clinic so that his baby brother could be treated for the dreaded Ricketts disease. 'She had to walk from Devonport, pushing him in a chair. Both his legs had been medically broken to correct the complaint. On one visit the pushchair was stolen from outside.'

The police station was adjacent, remembered Mr G.T. Kiddle of Whitleigh. He was serving on HMS *Revenge* and reported there when he was detailed for town patrol. 'We used to put drunken lads on the No. 14 bus to Drake where they would be put off by the conductors.'

Other readers variously remembered the building for its library, ballroom dancing , piano recitals, and the small area of grass next to it: 'It was next to a finely kept little park. No walking on the grass was allowed and a fine day would see all the seats occupied.'

~ *DEVASTATED AND CLOSE TO DESPAIR* ~

On 20th March 1941 the people of Plymouth, battered but unbowed, decked themselves out in their best finery and lined the streets to welcome the King and Queen to a city whose pre-war features were still clearly recognisable.

An air raid warden, standing on the ruins of his old house, waved his steel helmet at the passing cavalcade and shouted, 'We're keeping our chins up!'

'Yes, I can see you are,' the Queen replied, with that magnificent regal sweep of her hand, which is with her to this day.

The royal party, following an afternoon of golden sunshine, had left the city only three hours earlier – just after 6 p.m. – when the banshee wails from the sirens heralded the death-knell of the old city. Bombers, preceded by pathfinders, rained fire, destruction and death from the clear skies for more than four hours, methodically flying from east to west along three miles of the crescent that stretched between the Plym and the Tamar.

The royal visit had lifted drooping morale. It ended at Lord and Lady Astor's home in Elliot Terrace, on The Hoe, before driving through cheering crowds to North Road Station, a ramshackle barn of a terminus. Earlier the

Derry's Clock stands sentinel over the devastation.

royal couple had toured the large number of areas already devastated, chatting with many who had lost their homes and who, in some cases, were to have their lives suddenly snatched from them by enemy aircraft which cruised above them at will.

The bombs reduced whole districts to gaunt and blackened ruin. In the attack that night and the one which followed on the next night, 336 civilians were killed and Plymouth's compact heart was destroyed beyond repair. By the early hours of that second morning the city had been truly stricken: the business, commercial, entertainment and civic offices had been mostly gutted; some 20,000 properties were destroyed or damaged beyond repair.

That fine square enclosed by St Andrew's Church, the Guildhall, the modern Post Office and the Council Chamber had been devastated beyond belief, the dying embers spitting and hissing at the firemen who battled against hopeless odds.

Wave after remorseless wave of planes bombed Cattedown, Mutley, Stonehouse and the city centre. The fire was uncontrollable as furnishing and fabrics flared into the night, a beacon for the bombers. The whole area around St Andrew's Cross was a crackling inferno. Yet, unbelievably, even worse damage was to be inflicted on the following night.

'The fires are very much worse than in yesterday's attacks, and damage is even more extensive,' wrote one journalist in his war diary. Banks, clubs, churches and warehouses all became crumpled masses of rubble; Derry's

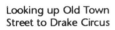
Looking up Old Town Street to Drake Circus

George Street –
a still-smoking ruin

Clock survived, almost a lone witness to the prewar city loved by so many. In those two nights something like the equivalent of one billion pounds' worth of real estate was wiped off the map of Plymouth.

Those who knew Plymouth before the war – and that included nearly every man in the Navy – could scarcely recognise the central areas. Even today, those familiar with its old layout are unable to walk through it without a quiver of memory; there is a wistful edge to its new image. Yet the death of a city had seemed unlikely to government officials. Gravely getting the likely scenario wrong, they had graded Plymouth as a neutral zone, little dreaming that France was to collapse so soon, thus giving the Germans airfields from which to bomb the south-west of England and Wales. Local MPs and leading citizens had warned Whitehall that such a great naval arsenal offered an irresistible target, but to no avail. Not until children died in their hundreds did Whitehall hastily revise its ideas and consent to it being designated an evacuation area, whereupon 12,000 youngsters left for the small towns of Devon and Cornwall.

Winston Churchill came down and the macabre sight which greeted him brought tears to his eyes. In one of his immortal phrases, he shouted from the back of an open Daimler, 'Your homes are low but your hearts are high.' This was not good enough for Lady Astor who, later that day, told him over

These wooden huts at Mount Batten were part of RAF 19 Group, under Coastal Command, and the met offices.

tea and crumpets at Elliot Terrace, 'It's all very well to cry, Winston, but you've got to do something.'

It was a bit late. By the end of April the record of loss was overwhelming: practically every pub, 3,000 houses, twenty schools, 39 churches and chapels, six hotels and over 100 inns had gone. The five attacks in April, mainly targeted on the Devonport end, combined more than twenty-three hours of continuous bombardment. The great fires provided the stimulus which brought the National Fire Service to birth, but that came too late to save a city where the pumps rushed in by visiting brigades would not even fit the hydrants and lay coiled in the streets, inert and useless.

Yet, with it all, the people of Plymouth took recourse to their ancient 'shrine', The Hoe, and there they danced. While their city lay battered across its hills, a dance band from the Army Pioneer Corps played for two hours each night. Tired as they were, people came in crowds. Lady Astor often led the dance with a serviceman, and one picture of her doing so was flashed around the world.

People also went in crowds to bathe; one night 3,000 of them bought tickets for Tinside. And, somewhere or other, there was always the reassuring sight of the tall, slightly stooping Lord Astor, usually accompanied by his vivacious wife, golden lorgnettes swinging from her bosom, and always one for the wisecrack.

And what of the people who endured it all – those who didn't pack their bags and move elsewhere for the duration? After those two terrible nights in March they were, wrote H.P. Twyford, 'hollow-eyed for want of sleep, with vengeance and hatred in their hearts against the perpetrators of total war'. Perhaps that was rather overstating the situation, written, as it was, in the fierce heat of battle. Many Plymothians were numbed, emotionally drained and near to despair; some became hysterical. Deep scars had been sustained before during the city's long and tumultuous history, but this seemed like the final funeral dirge. Its apocalyptic horror had, after all, followed thirty-one raids of varying intensity.

But many of them, like their city, survived; this had always been the case. Plymouth lives with its ghosts. It is, as J.C. Trewin wrote, 'at once proud, haunted and inescapably romantic'. Given its history, is it any wonder that tragic overtones permeate its very atmosphere?

~ *THE PLAN FOR PLYMOUTH* ~

These five earnest men, peering at the model of future Plymouth, are the leading figures involved in the city's post-war reconstruction. From left to right they are: the Town Clerk; Sir Colin Campbell, joint author of the Plymouth Plan; Professor Patrick Abercrombie the great town planner; the Lord Mayor, Lord Astor; the City Engineer J. Paton Watson; and the Deputy Lord Mayor, Alderman W.J. Modley.

Sometime derided for their lack of vision in the redevelopment of the city, it is forgotten by many that lack of money prevented these men from putting the whole of their ambitious plan into action.

Key figures in the planning of Plymouth's post war future.

~ *THE KING AND QUEEN IN PLYMOUTH* ~

On 29 October 1947 King George VI and Queen Elizabeth came to Plymouth to officially open Royal Parade and Armada Way, although both thoroughfares were still incomplete.

In the photograph the Queen is seen with the Lord Mayor of that time, Alderman Harry Taylor – slightly ironical in that he was a bitter opponent of the Watson-Abercrombie Plan and spoke forcefully against its implementation at city council meetings.

The date remains blazoned in Mrs Joan Rickard's mind. It was a very special day in Plymouth's post-war life, when the King and Queen paid a visit to the city, which was thronged by thousands of cheering spectators. King George VI unveiled the Drake Drum flagstaff and officially opened Royal Parade and Armada Way, then well under way.

'The Lord Mayor was Alderman Harry Taylor and my father, the late Alderman H.J. Perry, was the Lord Mayor elect; at that time mayor choosing was in November,' recalled Mrs Rickard.

Mr Freddie Knox of Salisbury Road, St Judes, mentioned that Alderman Taylor became First Citizen more by accident than design.

Queen Elizabeth, now the Queen Mother, visiting Plymouth

'In November 1946 the Conservatives on the city council unanimously decided that Alderman William Modley – who had so diligently served for five years as deputy to Lord Astor – should be honoured with the Lord Mayoralty. He later announced that he would appoint Harry Taylor as his deputy. Alas, fate stepped in for Alderman Modley was taken ill some weeks before Lord Mayor choosing day and, on medical advice, had to decline the offer, so Alderman Taylor took it.'

~ THE NEW ROYAL PARADE ~

Some of the buildings shown in this picture of Royal Parade in its early days are still standing today. Many readers had recollections of this scene, though only Des Leach mentioned the pawnbrokers Levy & Slogget, whose shop stood in splendid isolation on Derry's Cross roundabout when all around it was being either demolished or rebuilt.

He also pointed out that the small white building on the left of the Odeon cinema, near the top right-hand corner, was the old Barley Sheaf pub. This was not far from the *Evening Herald* office, the back of whose printing works is seen in the picture.

Formerly called the Regent, the Odeon cinema was one of the largest in the country at that time: it held over 3,000 people. Field Marshal Montgomery gave a 'pep' talk to high-ranking servicemen there not long before the D-Day landings.

The other large building overlooking Royal Parade was the former Co-operative Society premises, in Courtenay Street and Raleigh Street; the latter was the first street in which rebuilding took place, in March 1947.

The site was well remembered by Mr P.S. Biggs – he was born in one of the houses in Wembury Street, opposite the former Co-op building. He observed that the section of the Co-op building shown in the photograph, which stocked furniture, was all that was left of its massive premises after the bombing. However, it did include a cafe on the top floor, used for all kinds of functions, including tea dances.

Mr Jack Hallett remembered Courtenay Street only too well, for he used to walk it as a regular pitch when working as a junior clerk and messenger for the solicitors Whiteford, Bennett and Woolland. His job was to deliver correspondence to other solicitors, estate agents and commercial businesses. He was just thirteen and little guessed that he would stay with that old-established firm for fifty-two years, retiring in 1986 as assistant chief cashier.

Mr Hallett pointed out that the county assize court and the quarter sessions court met underneath the Guildhall's tower at the edge of the Square.

Royal Parade, soon
after its completion
in 1948

Many people will remember the Nissen huts, on the other side of Royal Parade, which served as temporary shop premises for many years. Also in the picture is the old railway bridge in Union Street, carrying the line that once served Millbay Station.

~ WHEN THE CUSTOMER WAS ALWAYS RIGHT ~

The photographs on the following page reminded many readers of how much more pleasant it was shopping in the city when the customer was not just another face at the till.

'You always felt that you mattered very much as a person, not just a customer,' recalled Mr Frederick of Mounts Gould Road.

Whipples, the butchers, triggered off memories for many; this was half way down on the right of the top picture opposite. The butcher and his wife were Ted and Maud Morrish who certainly drew fond memories from many *Herald* readers.

The scene near Old Town Street in the 1950s.

Julie Baker, née Jago, pictured in the pince-nez, purchased through Russell Capps in 1955.

Mr John Frederick was one such reader. He was an active member of the Christian Endeavour at the time the picture was taken in the 1950s, and Mr Morrish and his sister were leading lights in evangelical work.

'Ted Morrish unfailingly greeted everyone with a smile and a cheery word. He just oozed goodwill. He took a leading role in the relays to Plymouth of Billy Graham's 1954 meetings at the Harringay Arena, and those of us involved will never forget how well he handled them.'

Other reminscences were triggered by the sign above Russell Capps, the optician. Julie Baker, was a young lady at the time the above photograph was taken in 1955. 'I was prescribed a pair of pince-nez and they broke on

These shops at the top of York Street were demolished some time ago.

the afternoon that I first wore them. The thoroughly apologetic optician not only repaired them but offered to send me another spare pair within a week, which he did.'

'I was only twenty at the time but I have always remembered the courtesy and attention, by no means an isolated feature of business all those years ago. By this simple act of courtesy, Capps secured a customer for life, and I am now in my early sixties.'

Kenneth Hoppins easily spotted the location of the photograph as Old Town Street, because he worked in one of the shops there in 1940. He was an apprentice electrician employed by John Collister. He also pointed out an interesting link in that Spooners took over Collister's electrical business after that had moved to Salisbury Road, St Jude's.

Mr Hoppins also correctly identified the block of shops shown in the photograph above. They once stood at the top of York Street. Next door to Coop's Furniture Store was Warwick's which combined confectionery and tobacco sales with ladies and gents hairdressing.

✺ ✺ ✺

~ FROM COUGH CURES TO WATCH REPAIRS ~

Several readers who remembered the temporary market in the photograph below had good reason to do so; they worked there as shop assistants behind stalls run by such firms as Woolworth, Dolcis Shoe Company and Timothy White's.

Others, like Mr K.R. Endacott, had long association with the old market, seen in the picture. He pointed out that the Wholesale and Retail Meat Market, to give it its full title had its centre ripped out during the Blitz but that some of the perimeter buildings remained. Eventually those to the left of the gates were demolished to make way for the construction of New George Street.

'My family traded there since 1872 and continued throughout the war. After my release from the army, I took over the business, trading in two of the six shops then remaining inside the market gates. I continued until the opening of the new market in 1958 when my premises fronted on to new Cornwall Street.'

Taken just after the Second World War, this photograph shows a bustling scene in the old pannier market. In the early post-war years the market provided a welcome haven for shopkeepers who had been 'blitzed' out of their premises.

Rebuilding work in progress in the vicinity of the old market and the Corn Exchange, some five years after the war

Mr Endacott, of Beaumont Road, thought that the gates were finally transferred to Weston Mill cemetery for use there, though he was not sure if this actually happened.

Colleen Gaynor of Underwood Lane, Plymstock, recognised her uncle as the gentleman standing by the Woolworth's stall with his back to the camera. From Australia, Mrs Joan Petty wrote to say that she was also in the photograph, standing behind the Woolworth's counter, with her mother and younger sister in the crowd.

Patricia Weeks said that she worked for Marks & Spencer in the old pannier market. 'The summers were terribly hot because of the glass roof, and the winters very cold, so we were issued with donkey jackets and clogs to keep warm.'

Mrs B. Knight recalled that she spent many hours with her mother and small brother in the market. 'The fish ladies would be lined up with their white overalls and, in some cases, sack-cloth. 'On weekends we used to listen to the Salvation Army and the politicans on their soapboxes. My step-father used to spout for NUWM, and on Saturday nights the "Chocolate Kid" and others would be in action. However, the one who was the most fascinating to me was the man making "Ted's Cough-No-More" sweets, all by hurricane lamps in the winter, and whatever the weather.'

Referring to the second picture, Mr K. Hulse identified Coles tea-blending shop, with the meat market in between that and the Corn Exchange. 'The front corner of the picture is the Dudley Coles building site for part of the Norwich Union building and, on the opposite corner, work is about to start on Boots the chemists.'

Mr S. Robertson pointed out that the two scenes were only a few yards from each other. He said that the first picture shows the east entrance of the old market and the south entrance was Market Avenue. 'This area was a hive of activity well into the evenings and weekends. Pre-war traders had stalls there, well lit by portable gas lamps, and you could get most things from a cough cure to a watch repair in a matter of minutes.' Similar memories of this scene in Plymouth's history were recalled by many other people.

~ *TIN PAN ALLEY* ~

The picture of Tin Pan Alley, just outside the old market, was easily recognised by readers as a popular place for real bargains in a huge range of goods. One correspondent described the alley as 'galvanised shacks'; they were erected between the east entrance of the old market and the bottom of Saltash Street.

Tin Pan Alley, a popular shopping venue in the years immediately after the Second World War

The lady in the white coat, standing at the entrance, and the gentleman in the cap were recognised by John Reed as his mother and father. His mother, he said, 'was charged the princely sum of two shillings and sixpence a day. Fish dealers might like to know that in those days my sister was there at 6 a.m. and had sold one cart full of fish by the time my mother and father arrived three hours later with a second full cart. The carts were rented from Chapman's for sixpence a day. They had to pay a man to push the first cart full of fish and ice from the Barbican to Tin Pan Alley. Good old days?'

THE FOUNTAINS OF DRAKE'S PLACE RESERVOIR

Drake's Place Reservoir, at Sherwell Gardens, renovated and reopened to the public in recent years, has long been a favourite spot for Plymothians.

Mr Donald Chapman was one of many readers who recalled often spending a lunch break there. 'I sat, with others, under the covered arches, watching the traffic and the decorative water fountains.'

Mr Bennett of Chaddlewood Avenue remembered the shops opposite as being Foster's the boot repairers, Pooley's bakery shop and Underhill's the butchers, at the end of Armada Street, with a doctor's surgery on the opposite corner.

Mrs E. Jordan from Kingsbridge recalled that her father-in-law was the general foreman with the Plymouth City Waterworks and lived at the house in Endsleigh Place. 'He had the garden by the wall at the back of the picture, with marvellous results due partly to the spray from the fountains. His father used to be the park keeper in the gardens.'

Though the fountains no longer flow, the scene at Drake's Place Reservoir has changed little since this picture was taken

~ INDEX ~